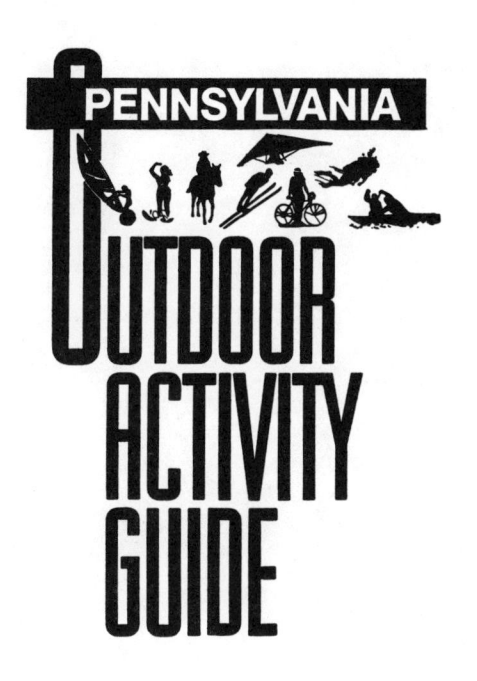

PENNSYLVANIA OUTDOOR ACTIVITY GUIDE

PENNSYLVANIA OUTDOOR ACTIVITY GUIDE

Sally Moore

Illustrated by Dale Ingrid Swensson

Country Roads Press
CASTINE · MAINE

Pennsylvania Outdoor Activity Guide
© 1995 by Sally Moore. All rights reserved.

Published by Country Roads Press
P.O. Box 286, Lower Main Street
Castine, Maine 04421

Text and cover design by Studio 3, Ellsworth, Maine.
Illustrations by Dale Ingrid Swensson.
Typesetting by Typeworks, Belfast, Maine.

ISBN 1-56626-111-2

Library of Congress Cataloging-in-Publication Data

Moore, Sally, 1936–
    Pennsylvania outdoor activity guide / author, Sally Moore ; illustrator, Dale Ingrid Swensson.
       p. cm.
    Includes index.
    ISBN 1-56626-111-2 : $9.95
    1. Outdoor recreation—Pennsylvania—Guidebooks.
    2. Pennsylvania—Guidebooks.   I. Title.
GV191.42.P4M66   1995
796.5'09748—dc20   94-39056
                                                                      CIP

Printed in the United States of America.
10 9 8 7 6 5 4 3 2 1

To Ryan and Caitlin

Walk in beauty

CONTENTS

Acknowledgments *ix*

Introduction *xi*

1 HIKING *1*

2 BICYCLING *32*

3 HORSEBACK RIDING *65*

4 PADDLE SPORTS *86*

5 FISHING *111*

6 BIRDING *135*

7 BALLOONING AND GLIDING *157*

8 SKIING *170*

9 SOURCES OF INFORMATION *189*

Index *200*

ACKNOWLEDGMENTS

Whether knee-deep in a trout stream, careening over Youghiogheny rapids, or skiing through winter-stilled woods in the name of research, I owe my first debt of gratitude to the state of Pennsylvania, so rich in natural attributes that it made investigation a pleasure.

Second, I'd like to thank all the state agencies that responded to my interminable and explicit questions with patient forbearing: the Fish and Boat Commission, the Game Commission, the Department of Environmental Resources's Bureau of State Parks and Bureau of State Forests, the Department of Transportation, and last but certainly not least, the Bureau of Travel Marketing and the tourist promotion agencies throughout the state.

A debt of gratitude must be paid to Tom Thwaites, who first introduced me to the pleasures of Pennsylvania's hiking trails; to Tom Helm of the Bicycling Federation of

Pennsylvania, Tom Sexton of the Pennsylvania Rails-to-Trails Conservancy, and Dave Bachman, Pedestrian and Bicycling Coordinator, PennDOT, for their assistance in the cycling chapter; and to Bob McDemus for the lowdown on those high-flying hang-glider pilots.

Finally, a simple benediction to my husband, Dick, who not only supported this effort but saw to it that body and soul were kept together during the compilation of these chapters.

INTRODUCTION

In the woods we return to reason and faith.
                              —Ralph Waldo Emerson

All of us have special places where we find renewal and refreshment. As today's pace accelerates and living spaces become more and more congested, we have to get away, release our accumulated energies, and renew our acquaintance with the open spaces that nourished the spirits of our pioneer ancestors. Whether this involves a hike in the woods or fishing a limestone stream, Pennsylvania can oblige.

To those accustomed to thinking in terms of the state's most famous cities—Philadelphia or Pittsburgh—the broad intervening open expanses may come as a surprise. But to anyone who's seen the wild and rocky ridges of the south central region, the vast wooded spaces of the Alleghenies, or the faraway fringes of the Laurel Highlands, the outdoor opportunities are evident.

In truth, Pennsylvania's 45,333 square miles encompass almost every geographical feature except desert and ocean. Mountains divide the land into three regions. The Appalachian Plateau, which runs from Wayne County in the northeast to Somerset County in the southwest, is a place of high, flat-topped divides cut by stream-etched valleys. To the east and south of the plateau country, long, narrow mountain ridges and valleys make up the Appalachian Mountain section. Southeast of the mountains lies the Great Valley, running diagonally from Northampton to Franklin Counties. That's a lot of country for the outdoor enthusiast, more than enough to ensure that the crowds you've fled haven't followed you along.

For those familiar with the state, most locales do not need definition. For the newcomer, however, we have divided Pennsylvania into six geographic regions: the northeast, with the Pocono Mountain region, the Endless Mountains, and most of the coal country; the southeast, with Philadelphia and neighboring Bucks County, Valley Forge, and the Brandywine Valley; north central, with the greater portion of Allegheny National Forest; south central, with the valleys of the Susquehanna and the rolling homelands of the Pennsylvania Dutch; the northwest, with its lakes and rivers; and the southeast, with Pittsburgh and the Laurel Highlands.

This guide has been written to give you a sampling of the Commonwealth's potential, but it's just a portion of the possibilities. We've concentrated on those activities you can enjoy alone, with your family, or as part of a small group. Trying to be comprehensive without being encyclopedic,

Introduction

we've eliminated team and spectator sports, golf, tennis, and hunting.

Each chapter deals with a particular activity—accompanied by tips on getting the best experience and any applicable state or local regulations. Also given are the addresses and phone numbers of state and national outfitters, liveries, and purveyors of maps. We have attempted to present as much information as possible, but a listing should not be construed as an endorsement of any particular enterprise. For hours and costs, we suggest you contact the individual operations, as these factors change too frequently to be practical in a volume such as this.

Although care has been taken to obtain correct data as of the publication date of this guide, small business operations are variable and subject to amendment in hours, location, and vitality. If you detect a modification in a listing, we would consider it a service if you would contact the publisher, Country Roads Press, with the details.

In the case of club listings, administrators and addresses vary from year to year, but frequently previous officers can give you current contacts. In a constructive move, more and more clubs are renting permanent post office boxes to correct this problem. In any event, an advance phone call takes but a moment and forestalls disappointment.

The author has participated in many, but certainly not all, activities listed in this book. The reader no doubt will recognize those areas where we speak from the heart. When lack of practical expertise has arisen, we've talked with those experts who could best counsel the reader.

Finally, remember that our natural resources are fragile; once lost, they are difficult to renew. It has been a hard lesson to learn, and parts of Pennsylvania's landscape still suffer the scars of exploitation. Before William Penn, Pennsylvania's caretakers were Native Americans, who treated the land with respect and a realization that they were not lords of the land but merely a part of the great cycle of its life. We can do no better than emulate their example.

1 HIKING

Pennsylvania means Penn's Woods. It comes as a surprise to those acquainted only with the metropolitan centers of Philadelphia and Pittsburgh that 58 percent of the state is forested and 26 percent of those lands is in public ownership. This is the largest percentage of public forest land of any state in the eastern United States.

Although other locales may have received more renown, Pennsylvania has thousands of miles of uncelebrated footpaths where you can walk all day on a warm spring weekend and not meet another soul. The variety of experience is overwhelming: ridge trails; lowland meadow trails; trails along rivers, creeks, and streams; marsh trails; trails through stands of virgin forest; even a trail through a remnant of prairie. You'll find nature preserves, a national forest, a national recreation area, 114 state parks, state forests, and state game lands. You'll discover a state preserving the heritage of great naturalists and conservationists such as John Bartram, John James Audubon, and Gifford Pinchot, head of the Forest Service under President Theodore Roosevelt.

Pennsylvania's signed and guided trails are usually a result of cooperation between hiking clubs, conservation groups, and state agencies. Maps and guides come from a variety of sources and are often the result of the combined efforts of the involved organizations.

THE TOP TRAILS

Appalachian Trail

Pennsylvania is favored with a extended section of the famed Appalachian Trail, and there's no better place to get an impression of the track's South Mountain segment than the stretch between the Appalachian Trail Conference regional office in Boiling Springs and the crossing at Whiskey Springs Road. This 5.7-mile hike provides an excellent sampling of the trail's attractions, with its varied terrain, interesting geology, and valley views.

Start in downtown Boiling Springs at the ATC field office, where you're likely to meet other hikers resting, chatting with staff, or stoking up on supplies at the convenience store across the street. Take time to stroll the eastern edge of Children's Lake and watch the latest hatch of ducklings learning the ropes from their mother. At the pond's lower end, you can investigate the old iron furnace, which provided shot for Washington's army, or observe the anglers casting for trout in the Yellow Breeches, one of the East's premier trout streams.

Cross the old triple-arch stone bridge, pass the burned-out pallet factory, and meander along the valley floor. You hike through fields planted in season with corn, alfalfa, and wheat, then cross Leidigh Road and head into the woods to ascend South Mountain, the last outpost of the Blue Ridge chain. Climbing gradually, you reach Center Point Knob, once the trail's north-south midpoint, then dip down through the hardwoods, crossing an orange-blazed trail that leads to Boy Scout Camp Tuckahoe 1.7 miles to the left and YMCA Camp Minqua a half mile to the right.

In the hollow you ford Little Dogwood Run—an evergreen stream which can course high during spring runoff—and take a long climb to the next ridge, passing evidence of early charcoal hearths. The remaining distance to Whiskey Springs is a gentle series of slopes and inclines. Before reaching the road, you come to a massive rock outcropping, fine for observation of the surrounding woodlands or a spot for a leisurely lunch.

One of the prime attractions of this stretch of trail is its varied geology. South Mountain's rocks are the oldest you'll encounter in Pennsylvania, ranging in age from about 680 to 560 million years. Bedrock is vitreous quartzite (the region's "White Rocks"), phyllite, graywacke, metamorphosed volcanic rocks and conglomeratic quartzite—a rock you'll find near Whiskey Springs—which is reminiscent of the "pudding stone" of northwestern New Jersey.

When you reach Whiskey Springs, a true, ever-running mountain wellhead, you can end your hike or continue south toward Pine Grove Furnace State Park.

This short trek is but a small sample of the Appalachian Trail, which in its entirety runs 2,155 miles from Mount Katahdin, Maine, to Springer Mountain, Georgia. Pennsylvania's 232.3 miles follow the Blue Ridge from Pen Mar in Franklin County to the Delaware Water Gap in Monroe County. Rich in history, the trail winds through early Indian country, stretches of coal mining country, and remnants of the iron industry, which flourished from 1740 to post–Civil War times.

To trace the trail's Pennsylvania journey from northeast to southwest, let's follow it from the Delaware River, from which it climbs more than 1,100 feet from riverbed to the summit of Mount Minsi, then lines the ridgetop, periodically descending into wind and water gaps. Along the way it passes state game and forest lands, the holdings of the national park service, and Hawk Mountain Sanctuary, a 2,200-acre wildlife refuge on a major raptor flyway. If you can tear yourself away from the spring and fall spectacle of thousands of hawks, eagles, and osprey soaring overhead, you can visit the nearby Pinnacle, one of the most spectacular overlooks in Pennsylvania.

From this point, the trail again follows the pattern of ridge climbs and gap descents. Entering the great Cumberland Valley and climbing tabletop South Mountain outside Boiling Springs, it penetrates Michaux State Forest, passes Pine Grove Furnace and Caledonia State Parks, and arrives in Maryland at Pen Mar.

The varied geography evident in the Boiling Springs/ Whiskey Springs portion continues throughout Pennsylvania. There are constantly changing vistas and new challenges, with the northern reaches' long, narrow ridges broken by wind or water gaps; the middle section, with its fertile limestone soil and bosky streams; and the South Mountain area, with its gentle knobs rising from 550 to 1,190 feet above the valley floor.

Golden Eagle Trail

Ask any avid traveler of Keystone trails to name the state's top five hikes, and Golden Eagle will number among them. The 8.9-mile trail has it all: soaring vistas along the Pine Creek watershed, plentiful wildlife (watch for bear signs—deep scratches and missing bark on tree trunks), and open fields. Its route lies through state game lands, Wolf Run Wild Area, and Tiadaghton State Forest. The 2,100-foot vertical rise is perfect for a good workout without exhaustion, and the trail is a loop, so transportation is not a problem.

Because the Golden Eagle is on game land, overnight camping is not permitted. However, the Inn at Cedar Run is convenient not only to the Golden Eagle but to other trails, such as the Black Forest. Stan and Charlotte Dudkin run this gathering place for all types of outdoor enthusiasts, from cyclists to fishermen. Their rooms are comfortable, and their table is bounteous enough for the most famished hiker.

The trailhead is nearby, off State 414 north of the village of Cammal. To begin the ramble, cross the railroad tracks and look for the blazes leading up over a ledge. The surface is rough and irregular, so hiking boots are the footwear of choice.

At the start you follow Wolf Run, eventually crossing it on a bridge. As you continue up the stream, you have frequent crossings, and there is evidence of the logging activity earlier in the century. You'll be able to distinguish log skids and the remains of a logging camp, indicated by a stand of large evergreens and the carcass of an old camp stove.

Continuing up the ridge, you cross into state game land. From this highest point on the trail, you have a spectacular view of the fields of Beulahland to the east and Bonnell Run and the Black Forest to the west.

Hiking down the saddle, you follow Bonnell Run, climb the slope to Clark's Pasture, and follow an abandoned quarry road for a strenuous climb to a ridge with views of Wolf Run and Pine Creek. A series of steep switchbacks leads you off the ridge, into Wolf Run, and eventually back to your point of origin.

OTHER MAJOR AND WELL-KNOWN TRAILS

Baker and Rachel Carson Trails

The Baker Trail begins in Schenley on the Allegheny River, northeast of Pittsburgh in Armstrong County. It runs 140.6 miles north through Crooked Creek State Park, the Mahoning Creek Reservoir area, and Cook Forest, joining the North Country Trail in Allegheny National Forest. The trail and nine Adirondack-style shelters are maintained by the Pittsburgh Council of the American Youth Hostels.

A southern 34-mile extension, named the Rachel Carson Trail, passes near the birthplace of the environmentalist in Springdale and follows the heights of the Allegheny River. Starting at Harrison Hills Regional Park near Freeport on the river, it veers south and west, crosses the Pennsylvania Turnpike, and terminates at Allegheny County's North Park Beaver Shelter.

Hiking

Black Forest Trail System

One of Pennsylvania's great trail systems, the 42.2-mile Black Forest Trail is located in the northwest corner of Lycoming County near the town of Slate Run, on Pine Creek. Other than superb scenery with spectacular overlooks, this rugged track offers a profusion of loop trails to tempt the most avid hiker: the George Will Trail, the Ruth Will Trail, the 12.6-mile Sentiero DiShay, the Highland Hardwood Trail, and the Pine Bog Trail. In addition, there are multiple connecting paths, including Old Supply and Baldwin Gas Line Trails, and access to the Susquehannock Trail through the North and South Link Trails.

Named for the dense evergreen forests that once blanketed the area, the trail begins and ends in a pine plantation on a state forestry road west of State 414 near Slate Run.

Bucktail Path

The 32-mile Bucktail Path originates in Sizerville State Park, in Cameron County, and runs south through varied terrain and the Johnson Run National Area, a 200-acre preserve of old-growth hemlocks and hardwoods. It terminates in the village of Sinnemahoning.

Chuck Keiper Trail

In Sproul State Forest, the Chuck Keiper Trail is divided into two loops, east and west, with the northern part of

State 144 bisecting both portions. Named for a district game protector of western Clinton County, the 52.8-mile double loop crosses the Burns Run and Fish Dam Wild Areas, East Branch Swamp, and Cranberry Swamp Natural Areas. The 33.7-mile western loop and the 22.3-mile eastern loop are suitable for two- or three-day backpacking trips. Due to many stream crossings without bridges, it's best to hike this trail when there is low water.

Conestoga Trail

If you'd like to see historic Lancaster County but can't imagine hanging out the window of a car or tour bus, then you might enjoy the 65-mile Conestoga Trail, which routinely follows Hammer, Cocalico, Conestoga, and Pequea Creeks to the Susquehanna River and Lock 12 in York County.

The trail's northern terminus joins the Horse-Shoe Trail around Speedwell Lake, passes through fields and farmland, by old mills, covered bridges, and historic homes, and connects to the Mason-Dixon Trail at Lock 12 Historic Area on the west side of the Susquehanna near State 74. The last 15 miles are in the river hills and through Pequea Creek Recreation Area along the gorge of Lake Alfred, a wide section of the river.

Darlington Trail

Another south central trail is the 10-mile Darlington Trail, which was an alternate to the Appalachian Trail during World War II, when military operations at Fort Indiantown

Hiking

Gap curtailed free passage. The trail starts at Sterretts Gap on State 34 and follows the top of Blue Mountain, crossing Miller's and Lamb's Gaps and ending near the fire tower off Tower Road in Rye Township.

This old footpath, which predates the Appalachian Trail, was named for an early missionary to the area. Recent development on Blue Mountain has put the trail's future in jeopardy. Before planning a hike, check to determine its condition.

Donut Hole Trail

According to north woods wisdom, the Donut Hole Trail was named because there is nothing in the middle of a donut, and no civilization is what you find along this path. Passing through the northern portion of Sproul State Forest, the 55.7-mile trail is accessed in the east off State 120 at Hyner Run State Park, proceeds in a southwesterly direction, and ends on State 120 between Sinnemahoning and Renovo. A section of the Susquehannock Trail connects the eastern and western portions of the Donut Hole Trail.

Forbes Road Historic Trail

If you're a history buff, you will relish this trail, which follows portions of the road cleared by Gen. John Forbes during the French and Indian War. The road was originally constructed to allow military passage to the forks of the Ohio, where the British clashed with the French and their Indian allies.

Pennsylvania Outdoor Activity Guide

The 29-mile trail extends from Cowans Gap State Park in Fulton County to Ray's Hill on the Bedford County line. It covers varied terrain, including country roads, a telephone cable line, and a section of paved State 522. It is maintained by the Boy Scouts of America (BSA), and there are shelter cabins near the midpoint at BSA Camp Sinoquipe near Fort Littleton.

Glacier Ridge Trail

Part of the proposed North Country Trail running from Vermont to North Dakota, Glacier Ridge is located in Moraine State Park. Beginning near the north shore bike rental, the trail continues 9 miles northeast to Jennings Environmental Education Center near State 8.

Horse-Shoe Trail

A play on words, the Horse-Shoe Trail was named for its designated use as both an equestrian and a hiking path. History buffs especially will relish this route, which begins in Valley Forge National Historical Park and winds northwest through French Creek State Park near Hopewell Furnace National Historical Site, an early American ironmaking community. The 130.1-mile trail curves through five counties before joining the Appalachian Trail near the Dehart Dam, northeast of Harrisburg.

John P. Saylor Memorial Trail

Named for a western Pennsylvania congressman and conservationist, the John P. Saylor Memorial Trail is a double loop through the Babcock Division of Gallitzin State Forest

Hiking

in northeastern Bedford County. Four of the total 17.3 miles pass Clear Shade Wild Area. A smaller, complementary loop of 6 miles is accessed by a swinging bridge near the spot where the main trail passes the north bank of Clear Shade Creek.

Laurel Highlands Hiking Trail

Linear and fragmented Laurel Ridge State Park spans four counties and stretches along Laurel Mountain from the Youghiogheny River at Ohiopyle to the Conemaugh Gorge near Johnstown. The 70-mile Laurel Highlands Hiking Trail generally follows the contours of the 2,700-foot-high mountain but occasionally dips to the valley floor to cross portions of the high plateau in Fayette and Somerset Counties.

The trail has been kept as primitive as possible, with development only in areas where roads cross the ridge. Every eight to ten miles there are five Adirondack-type, three-sided shelters and tent pads with water supply and comfort stations.

Adapted to all-season use, the Laurel Highlands Trail has something to suit the day hiker, the end-to-end backpacker, the cross-country skier, snowshoer, and winter hiker.

Lost Turkey Trail

Built in 1973 by the Youth Conservation Corps in cooperation with numerous state agencies, the 26.2-mile Lost Turkey Trail won its name because during its construction several experienced woodsmen became "temporarily disoriented."

The 26.2-mile trail covers some rough terrain, and

hikers should be in good physical condition to attempt it. Its northeastern trailhead is near the fire tower in Blue Knob State Park in Bedford County, and it ends at Babcock picnic area off State 56 in Gallitzin State Forest.

Loyalsock Trail

The 59.3-mile Loyalsock Trail is another candidate for "the best of Pennsylvania hiking trails." It passes parts of Tiadaghton and Wyoming State Forests, Worlds End State Park, and several bosky waterfalls.

A "wilderness footpath" running from State 87, ten miles north of Montoursville, to US 220 north of Laporte, the trail generally parallels the Loyalsock Creek. With its source in Wyoming County, the waterway eventually empties into the Susquehanna River, its winding course providing the hiker and backpacker with beautiful vistas.

Mason-Dixon Trail

Traversing the woods and fields of south central and southeast Pennsylvania, eastern Maryland, and Delaware, the 182.7-mile Mason-Dixon Trail combines back roads and back-country walking with a tour through a historic section of the mid-Atlantic.

The northern terminus is the Brandywine Trail in Chadds Ford, Pennsylvania, home of the well-known Wyeth family. The route then heads south to Iron Hill Park, near Newark, Delaware, and continues through Elk Neck State Park. At Havre de Grace, Maryland, it follows the west bank of the Susquehanna for 65 miles to Wrightsville,

Hiking

Pennsylvania, finally joining the Appalachian Trail at Whiskey Springs, near Mount Holly Springs.

Mid State Trail System

The magic of the Mid State lies not only in its length (172 miles) but in its more than 70 side trails, which provide many opportunities for circuit hikes. From its northern terminus at the West Rim Trail of Pine Creek Gorge on Bohen Run north of Blackwell, it winds south to US 22 between the villages of Water Street and Alexandria. Generally maintaining a ridge profile through central Pennsylvania, the track is rarely far from civilization yet provides an illusion of wilderness.

Almost entirely on public land, it intersects two scout camps, three wild areas, four state forests, eight state parks, eight natural areas, and Stone Valley Recreation Area. It passes through the town of Woolrich, home to the well-known clothing manufacturer.

There are camping sites at Greenwood Furnace, Penn Roosevelt, Poe Valley, Poe Paddy, Reeds Gap, R.B. Winter, and Little Pine State Parks as well as primitive camping in many areas along the way.

North Country National Scenic Trail

The North Country Trail in Pennsylvania traverses 180 miles from Willow Bay Recreation Area one mile south of the New York border on the eastern shore of Allegheny Reservoir to the Ohio border west of McConnells Mill State Park. It is part of the National Trails System's North

Country Trail, which will eventually link Lake Sakakawea State Park on the Missouri River in North Dakota to Crown Point, New York.

On its course it passes the gorge of Slippery Rock Creek, joins the Glacier Ridge Trail in Moraine State Park, and heads northeastward, paralleling parts of the Allegheny and Clarion Rivers. Joining and following the Baker Trail, the path leads through Cook Forest State Park and state forest lands. The 95-mile segment through 500,000-acre Allegheny National Forest crisscrosses old logging trails, utility rights-of-way and abandoned railroad grades.

Old Loggers Path

A 27.1-mile circuit trail in northeast Lycoming County, the Old Loggers Path is true to its name, following retired railroad grades, logging roads, and bark trails. Its trailhead is 2.7 miles southwest of Ellenton on Legislative 4110. It passes through land formerly belonging to the Central Pennsylvania Lumber Company, now state forest.

Pinchot Trail System

Constructed by the Northeast Pennsylvania Sierra Club, the 25-mile Pinchot Trail System loops over the varied ridges, creeks, and swamps of the Pocono Plateau. Painter Creek and Choke Creek areas are especially appealing, and a side trail leads to Pine Hill Tower Lookout, with a panoramic view of the surrounding countryside.

Hiking

Quehanna Trail

Another circuit track, the 73.7-mile Quehanna Trail passes through the 47,000-acre Quehanna Wild Area, connecting with the Donut Hole Trail and Bucktail Path through spurs. Set in sections of Moshannon and Elk State Forests, the trail begins and ends at Parker Dam State Park in northern Clearfield County.

Readers should know something of the history of this region before making a decision whether to hike or backpack here. The Quehanna has a checkered past, having served Curtis Wright as the site for highly secret atomic energy research in the 1950s. In the 1960s when the corporation discontinued its Quehanna operations, the small reactor built here was moved, but the area suffered additional abuse in the form of unregulated dumping of hazardous waste by other entities.

Pennsylvania's Department of Environmental Resources and the federal Nuclear Regulatory Commission are constantly monitoring special wells in the area. The agencies believe that the low-level radioactive waste once placed there no longer presents a danger to recreational users.

Susquehannock Trail System

Traversing the Hammersley Run Wild Area and connecting both to the Black Forest Trail through the South and North Link Trails and to the Donut Hole Trail, the 85-mile Susquehannock circuit splices old Civilian Conservation Corps (CCC) fire trails, logging roads, and railroad grades. This system is a particular favorite of Canadian hiking clubs; in the fall you will hear their hearty camaraderie on this north central footpath.

With access at the northern gateway off US 6 near Denton Hill Ski Area, the southern gateway off State 44/144 near Ole Bull State Park, and other intersecting points, the trail offers numerous opportunities to hike it in segments.

Thunder Swamp Trail System

In Pike County on the Pocono Plateau, the Thunder Swamp system consists of a 30-mile loop trail complemented by another 15 miles of side trails. As the name implies, the greater share of the path bridges wetlands, but other areas are quite rocky. Stream crossings are frequent.

Situated in Delaware State Forest, the trail penetrates the Stillwater and Fennel Run Natural Areas. It is accessed by leaving I-84 at exit 8 and taking State 402 south for 14 miles.

Tuscarora Trail

The Tuscarora Trail–Big Blue is a 220-mile bypass of the Appalachian Trail in Pennsylvania, Maryland, West Virginia, and Virginia. The complete trail's northern end is at the junction of the Appalachian and Darlington Trails near Dean's Gap, west of the Susquehanna River at Harrisburg. It rejoins the Appalachian Trail in Shenandoah National Park in Virginia. The Tuscarora section ends near the C.&O. Canal towpath at the Potomac River in Hancock, Maryland.

The Pennsylvania portion of the route generally follows

the ridge top, with tough going in some of the northern regions. Gypsy moth caterpillar depredations have thinned the leaf canopy, resulting in more light reaching the forest floor and the inevitable brushy undergrowth. The situation has improved recently due to the vigilance of the Keystone Trail Association and the Potomac Appalachian Trail Club, but it's still a problem in some places.

Warrior Trail

One of the most ancient pathways in the East, the Warrior Trail is about 5,000 to 8,000 years old, a track for prehistoric hunters and gatherers to pass from the western banks of the Monongahela River to the shores of the Ohio. These days, the 67-mile-trail begins at Greensboro, Pennsylvania, passes westward to Cameron, West Virginia, and ends at Cresaps Bottom on the Ohio River below Moundsville, West Virginia. The trail can be accessed at numerous points along the way, and each mile is marked with a post emblazoned with "Warrior Trail" on the south exposure.

West Rim Trail

True to its name, the 30.2-mile West Rim Trail runs along the west side of Pine Creek Gorge, through Tioga State Forest in northern Lycoming and Tioga Counties. Although most of the trail passes through heavily timbered areas, there are some good vistas along the way.

In the northern part, the intersecting Barbour Rock Trail, a popular day hike, has outstanding views of the gorge dubbed the "Grand Canyon of Pennsylvania." Where

Barbour Rock joins the West Rim Trail, there is an overlook of Owassee Rapids and the surrounding plateau.

The terrain is rich in wildlife. You may find traces of bear, and if you're stationary and quiet, a wild turkey hen may shepherd her small flock across your path.

The trail generally parallels a series of dirt roads (see *Country Roads of Pennsylvania*, Chapter 9, for the auto tour). The northern terminus is in Ansonia, a half mile south of US 6 on Colton Road; the southern end is on State 414, two miles south of Blackwell on Pine Creek. Here the northernmost section of the Mid State Trail joins the West Rim Trail at Bohen Run.

Although this is just a portion of what you can expect to encounter on Pennsylvania trails, we hope it will whet your appetite to discover the riches of Penn's Woods. Changes are constantly made to trail length, route, and general condition. It is always a good idea to check with the responsible agency to discover if a previously intact crossing has been swept away by high water or if a section of the path has been rerouted due to development in the area.

RAIL TRAILS

During the past quarter century, the emergence of automobiles and trucks as the preferred means of moving freight and people has sounded the death knell of many of the country's rail lines. For a time, these abandoned railroad grades lay fallow, until a group of concerned citizens realized that a valuable resource was being wasted. In 1985 the Rails-to-Trails Conservancy was established to "enhance America's communities and countrysides by

Hiking

converting thousands of miles of abandoned rail corridors, and connecting open space, into a nationwide network of public trails."

Nationally, almost 7,000 miles of rail-trails have been developed, and Pennsylvania has more than 700. These range from the Schuylkill River Trail near Philadelphia to the Pymatuning State Park Trail near the Ohio border. You can visit a deserted mining town on Ghost Town Trail near Nanty Glo in Cambria County, check out one of the East's most famous natural trout streams on the LeTort Spring Run Nature Trail near Carlisle, or catch a slice of transportation history at the Allegheny Portage Railroad Trail near Cresson. Trail length varies from the 48-mile Armstrong Trail in Clarion and Armstrong Counties to the half-mile trail over Warren County's Kinzua railroad bridge, the highest in the world when it was built in 1882. Trail surfaces range from the original ballast to asphalt, and some are wheelchair accessible.

Information on rail-trails appears in several chapters of this book, since many of the trails are multiple use, appealing equally to hikers, cross-country skiers, equestrians, cyclists, snowmobilers—even in-line and roller skaters. The guidebook *Pennsylvania's Great Rail-Trails* gives information on the use of each trail, its length, surface, history, highlights, and a contact agency or person.

ORIENTEERING

Compared with the ancient tradition of seeing the sights by shank's mare, orienteering is a new pursuit. Of Scandinavian origin, it is both a footrace and a puzzle—a treasure hunt and track meet combined.

With topographic map and compass, participants race

against the clock to locate markers in the woods and check in at these points or controls before crossing the finish line. Although everyone uses the same map, the means of navigation from control to control vary according to the skill of the players.

Courses range in length from one kilometer for beginners to fifteen kilometers for experts. They vary from place to place, and it takes great attention to detail and meticulous planning to stage an event. Although the sport can be extremely competitive, its intensity can be adjusted for all levels of expertise, from children to seniors.

State Orienteering Sites

Orienteering is an organized event. The sites listed below are but a few of the places events have been held. For information on current events, contact the appropriate club.

Evansburg State Park, Montgomery County
French Creek State Park, Berks County
Hickory Run State Park, Carbon County
King's Gap State Park, Cumberland County
Nottingham County Park, Chester County
Mont Alto State Park, Franklin County
Myrick Center (Brandywine Valley Association),
    West Chester, PA
Ridley Creek State Park, Delaware County
Rocky Ridge State Park, York County

Caveats

Although Pennsylvania has some of the most uncrowded trails in the East, you do share the path with others, seen

Hiking

or unseen, and common courtesy suggests that you "leave only footprints" and "take only pictures." This familiar phrase has some practical applications.

- Stay on the straight and narrow. Although bushwhacking can be fun—it brings out the explorer in us all—it is destructive to the native habitat. Avoiding those tiresome switchbacks and heading straight up is fine aerobic exercise, but the erosion you cause with your careless boot marks can destroy a hillside.
- Don't be a litterbug. Carry out what you carry in. In fact, if you're feeling particularly noble, you might try picking up after some less tidy hikers and campers as well.
- Respect the wildlife. The forest is home to the animals and birds. You are only a passing visitor. Observe but don't disturb.
- Plan your water supply. Carry your own, or boil available water for one minute, or use a portable purification unit. Even the clearest mountain stream may be host to a variety of unpleasant organisms.
- Maintain sanitary habits. Wash your person as well as cooking and eating utensils away from a water supply. Dump waste water at a distance. Use toilet facilities if provided; if none are available, with a trowel dig a "cat hole" eight to ten inches in diameter and no deeper than six to eight inches at least 200 feet from open water. Burn toilet paper and replace the soil.
- Be careful with fire. Use fireplaces at shelters or campsites, and never leave a fire unattended. Be sure it is completely out before departing the area. Even better, cook with a portable stove (dead wood can become scarce, and live wood won't burn). Fires are not permitted on state game lands, and other areas implement restrictions during times of fire hazard.

- Protect your vehicle against porcupines. They love salt and will chew on your car's cooling hoses, electrical wires, and brake and fuel lines. If you're parked at an out-of-the-way trailhead, deter the critters by scattering mothballs around your vehicle.
- Use extreme caution when hiking during hunting season. Pennsylvanians are avid deer hunters. The season is usually just after Thanksgiving until mid-December. Hunting is forbidden on Sundays.
- Beware of rabid animals. Rabies has become an increasing concern in recent years. If you come across an animal acting sick, sluggish, or in an uncharacteristic manner, avoid contact. If a hiker or pet is attacked by such an animal, seek immediate medical care.

FURTHER CAUTIONS

Although Pennsylvania abounds in wildlife, interaction between hikers, campers, and animals is rare. Of course, if you're careless with food storage and scrap disposal, you will probably be visited by freeloading skunks and raccoons.

There are three varieties of venomous snakes in the Commonwealth: the black-tailed timber rattlesnake, the Massasauga rattlesnake, and the northern copperhead. The Massasauga is endangered in Pennsylvania. A shy, retiring reptile, it is found in the western part of the state. Timber rattlers can generally be found on high, rocky, southern exposures; copperheads prefer rocky streambeds. The prudent hiker puts neither hand nor foot on trail or ledge without prior sight inspection.

Perhaps one of the least dangerous but most annoying

Hiking

aspects of Penn's Woods are biting insects. There are the usual mosquitoes, but the insect that wins the prize for irritation is what the locals call "gnats." It's actually a variety of black fly. When pollution was common in state waterways, these flies couldn't reproduce. Now that the streams have been cleaned up, the flies have returned. Hikers should be prepared with effective repellent.

CAMPING

There are two styles of campers: those who prefer the convenience and facilities of an established campground and those who want to be as far from civilization as their legs and stamina can carry them.

For the former, Pennsylvania's state parks provide campsites and cabins. A few areas are limited to tent camping only, but in most cases you will share with car campers, trailers, and motor homes.

For a simple campsite, you can check in at any of fifty-five state parks, with a total 7,000 available spots. The maximum length of stay is fourteen consecutive nights during the summer season. Pets and alcohol are not permitted; leashed dogs are permitted only in day-use areas.

Eleven state parks have cabins built in the 1930s of wood and stone. Kooser, Parker Dam, Linn Run, and Worlds End rent these rustic cabins year-round; the other seven parks lease from the second Friday in April until the Friday of the week of regular antlerless deer season. Fourteen state parks have modern cabins (read indoor plumbing); six parks offer year-round rentals of cottages, which vary in size and design.

Recreation opportunities in state parks range from

swimming, fishing, hiking, boating, and environmental education in the summer to cross-country skiing, snowshoeing, snowmobiling, and ice fishing in the winter.

For campsite rental, call the respective park office. Cabins are more difficult to secure; rentals go quickly when the Bureau of State Parks reservations open in late winter.

The camper who shuns the crowd will find primitive camping allowed on state forest lands and in Allegheny National Forest. Camping is **not** permitted on state game lands except where the Appalachian Trail crosses. Here a few Adirondack-type three-sided shelters exist.

You may camp along the Appalachian Trail if you stay within 200 feet of the trail, occupy a site for one night only, avoid camping within 500 feet of a water source or public access, and don't build open fires during times of fire hazard.

RESOURCES

Publications

Explore Pennsylvania's Grand Canyon, Chuck Dillon, Pine Creek Press, R.D. 4, Box 130B, Wellsboro, PA 16901; 717-724-3003. Fee.

Fifty Hikes in Central Pennsylvania and *Fifty Hikes in Western Pennsylvania*, Tom Thwaites, Backcountry Publications, P.O. Box 175, Department APC, Woodstock, VT 05091; 800-245-4151. Fee.

Fifty Hikes in Eastern Pennsylvania, Carolyn Hoffman, Backcountry Publications, P.O. Box 175, Department APC, Woodstock, VT 05091; 800-245-4151. Fee

Hiking

Hiking Guide to Western Pennsylvania, Bruce Sundquist and Cliff Ham, American Youth Hostels (AYH), Pittsburgh Council, Publishing Committee, 6300 Fifth Avenue, Pittsburgh, PA 15232; 412-422-2282. Fee.

Pennsylvania Hiking Trails, Keystone Trails Association (KTA), P.O. Box 251, Cogan Station, PA 17728-0251. Fee.

The Short Hiker, Jean Aron, 227 Kimport Avenue, Boalsburg, PA 16827. Short, easy hikes in central Pennsylvania. Fee.

WPC Outing Guides, Western Pennsylvania Conservancy, 316 Fourth Avenue, Pittsburgh, PA 15222; 412-288-2777. Series of guides to the seventy-five conservancy properties. Membership required.

State Agencies

Pennsylvania Department of Environmental Resources (DER)
Bureau of Forestry
Box 8552
Harrisburg, PA 17105-8552
717-783-7941
Public-use maps of roads and trails in state forests (or individual district headquarters).

Pennsylvania Game Commission
2001 Elmerton Avenue
Harrisburg, PA 17110-9797
717-783-7507

Pennsylvania Outdoor Activity Guide

Pennsylvania Department of Environmental Resources
Bureau of State Parks
P.O. Box 8551
Harrisburg PA 17105-8551
800-63 PARKS

Specific Trails

Appalachian Trail
Appalachian Trail Conference (ATC)
P.O. Box 807
Harpers Ferry, WV 25425

For a guidebook (fee) to the Pennsylvania section, contact:
Keystone Trails Association
P.O. Box 251
Cogan Station, PA 17728-0251

For specific trail conditions, contact:
ATC, Mid-Atlantic Regional Office
P.O. Box 381, 4 East First Street
Boiling Springs, PA 17007
717-258-5771

Baker Trail and Rachel Carson Trails
AYH, Pittsburgh Council
Publishing Committee
6300 Fifth Avenue
Pittsburgh, PA 15232
412-422-2282

Hiking

Black Forest Trail System
DER, Bureau of Forestry,
  Tiadaghton District
423 East Central Avenue
South Williamsport, PA
  17701
717-327-3450

Bucktail Path
DER, Bureau of Forestry
R.D. 1, Route 155, Box 327
Emporium, PA 15834
814-486-3353

Chuck Keiper Trail
DER, Bureau of Forestry
HCR 62, Box 90
Renovo, PA 17764
717-923-1450 or
  717-923-1458

Conestoga Trail
Lancaster Hiking Club
P.O. Box 6037
Lancaster, PA 17603
Robert Reisinger
  717-394-2457 after
  6 P.M.

Darlington Trail
Susquehanna Appalachian
  Trail Club
P.O. Box 61001
Harrisburg, PA 17106-1001

Donut Hole Trail
DER, Bureau of Forestry
HCR 62, Box 90
Renovo, PA 17764
717-923-1450 or
  717-923-1458

Forbes Road Historic Trail
Boy Scouts of America,
  Mason-Dixon Council
P.O. Box 2133
Hagerstown, MD 21742
301-739-1211

Glacier Ridge Trail
AYH, Pittsburgh Council
Publishing Committee
6300 Fifth Avenue
Pittsburgh, PA 15232
412-422-2282

Golden Eagle Trail
DER, Bureau of Forestry,
  Tiadaghton District
423 East Central Avenue
South Williamsport, PA
  17701
717-327-3450

Pennsylvania Outdoor Activity Guide

Horse-Shoe Trail
Horse-Shoe Trail Club
Robert L. Chalfant
509 Cheltena Avenue
Jenkintown, PA 19045
215-887-1549

*John P. Saylor
 Memorial Trail*
DER, Bureau of Forestry
P.O. Box 506, 131 Hillcrest
 Drive
Ebensburg, PA 15931
814-472-1862

*Laurel Highlands
 Hiking Trail*
Laurel Ridge State Park
R.D. 3, Box 246
Rockwood, PA 15557
412-455-3744
For a comprehensive
 guide, write:
Sierra Club of Pittsburgh
Ms. J. Apone
5228 Beeler Street
Pittsburgh, PA 15217

Lost Turkey Trail
DER, Bureau of Forestry
P.O. Box 506, 131 Hillcrest
 Drive
Ebensburg, PA 15931
814-472-1862

Loyalsock Trail
Williamsport Alpine Club
P.O. Box 501
Williamsport, PA 17703

Mason-Dixon Trail System
719 Oakbourne Road
West Chester, PA 19382

Mid State Trail System
Mid-State Trail Association
P.O. Box 167
Boalsburg, PA 16827
814-466-6067

North Country Trail
Pennsylvania Bureau of
 State Parks
P.O. Box 8551
Harrisburg, PA 17105-8551
800-63-PARKS

Pittsburgh Council,
 American Youth
 Hostels, Inc. (AYH)
6300 Fifth Avenue
Pittsburgh, PA 15232
412-362-8181

Allegheny National Forest
P.O. Box 847
Warren, PA 16365
814-723-5150

Hiking

*North Country, Ice Age, and Lewis and Clark
   National Trails*
700 Ray-O-Vac Drive, Suite 100
Madison, WI 53711-2476
608-264-5610

Old Loggers Path
DER, Bureau of Forestry, Tiadaghton District
423 East Central Avenue
South Williamsport, PA 17701
717-327-3450

Pinchot Trail System
DER, Bureau of Forestry
401 Samters Building, 101 Penn Avenue
Scranton, PA 18503
717-963-4561 or 717-963-4564

Quehanna Trail
Commonwealth of Pennsylvania
DER, Bureau of Waste Management
Harrisburg, PA 17120 (cleanup updates)
DER, Bureau of Forestry
P.O. Box 952
Clearfield, PA 16830
814-765-3741 or 814-765-8713 (trail maps)

Susquehannock Trail System
Susquehannock Trail Club
P.O. Box 643
Coudersport, PA 16915

Thunder Swamp
Trail System
DER, Bureau of Forestry
474 Clearview Lane
Stroudsburg, PA
  18360-3002
717-424-3001

Tuscarora Trail
Keystone Trails
  Association
P.O. Box 251
Cogan Station, PA
  17728-0251

Warrior Trail
Warrior Trail Association
c/o Lucille Phillips
R.D. 1, Box 35
Spraggs, PA 15362
412-451-8326

West Rim Trail
DER, Bureau of Forestry
Box 94, Route 287S
Wellsboro, PA 16901
717-724-2868
Pine Creek Press
R.D. 4, Box 130B
Wellsboro, PA 16901
717-724-3003 (complete
  trail guide and map, fee)

Rail Trails

Rails-to-Trails Conservancy, Pennsylvania Chapter
105 Locust Street
Harrisburg, PA 17101
717-238-1717
Pennsylvania's Great Rail-Trails, Tom Sexton and Julie Larison. Everything you need to know about Commonwealth rail trails. Fee.

Rails-to-Trails Conservancy
1400 Sixteenth Street NW, Suite 300
Washington, DC 20036
202-797-5400

Orienteering

Delaware Valley Orienteering Association
212 Westover Drive
Cherry Hill, NJ 08034

Indiana University of Pennsylvania Orienteering Club
c/o Tim Gilbert
110 Concord Street
Indiana, PA 15701
412-349-1408

Susquehanna Valley Orienteering Club
c/o Mike Ball
5587 Mercury Road
Harrisburg, PA 17109

U.S. Orienteering Federation
P.O. Box 1444
Forest Park, GA 30051

Warrior Ridge Orienteering Club
c/o Michael Lubich
P.O. Box 191
Rice's Landing, PA 15357
412-883-2238 after 6 P.M.

2 BICYCLING

With more miles of state-maintained roads than New York and the New England states combined, Pennsylvania offers the cyclist an almost unlimited variety of touring options. Whether it's the rolling Lancaster countryside or the precipitous terrain around the Allegheny Front, there is topography to please everyone, from the expert with legs of steel to the tyro just out for a jaunt.

Mountain bikers find the Commonwealth to their taste with the profusion of trails in state parks, forests, and game lands. In addition, the state's extensive rail-trails program supplies more than 700 miles of mixed-surface, nonvehicular paths, which may be shared by both touring bikes and mountain bikes. More miles are added every month as local volunteers strive to bring to reality the mission of the Rails-to-Trails Conservancy: enhancing America's communities and countrysides by converting abandoned rail corridors into a nationwide network of public trails.

Bicycling

PENNSYLVANIA RIDING REGULATIONS

Pennsylvania grants cyclists the same rights and responsibilities as any other driver on the road. You are respected as a legitimate user of the highway and are entitled to use a reasonable portion of the roadway without being endangered by other traffic.

Do's

- Ride with traffic on the right side of the road.
- Ride either on the right or left on one-way streets.
- Obey all traffic signs and signals and all rules of the road.
- Ride as close as possible to the edge of the traveled road.
- Use established bike paths within highway rights-of-way.
- Yield to pedestrians.
- Have at least one hand on the handlebar at all times.
- Equip children five years and under with ANSI or Snell Memorial Foundation standard helmets when they are riding in bike seats positioned over the rear wheel.
- Wear a helmet (they were not required at the time this guide was compiled, but their use is strongly suggested).
- Outfit your bike with a headlight visible for at least 500 feet, a rear reflector visible from 100 to 600 feet, and amber reflectors on the sides for night riding.
- Have brakes capable of stopping from fifteen miles per hour within fifteen feet on dry, level pavement.

Don'ts

- Travel on Commonwealth interstates.
- Wear headphones, earphones, or any similar device that impairs hearing ability.

- Ride more than two abreast except on a bicycle lane or path.
- Ride on the sidewalk in a business district unless specifically permitted by a sign.

ROAD NUMBERING SYSTEM

The Pennsylvania Department of Transportation marks most east-west highways in even numbers and those running north-south in odd numbers. This rule is beggared by numerous exceptions.

All routes are marked approximately every half mile with ten-inch by ten-inch or ten-inch by eighteen-inch white "segment markers," carrying the letters "SR" and the route number in two- to four-digit figures. Beneath the route designation is the segment number, which on north-south highways begins in the south, and on east-west highways begins in the west.

STATE FOREST AND GAME LAND TRAILS

Bicycles are permitted on all forest roads statewide, including some that have been gated to keep out motorized vehicles. The only prohibited trails are forestry-designated hiking trails. Cyclists may camp overnight along forestry trails *with a permit only.*

All state game land roads are open to cyclists during daylight hours; unlike forest lands, no overnight camping is allowed.

Bicycling

STATE PARK TRAILS

Many of Pennsylvania's 114 state parks have areas where cyclists are welcome to share multiuse paths. Parks with trails closed to cyclists generally are well signed. Maps are available by writing individual park offices of the Department of Environmental Resources (DER), Bureau of State Parks.

Of the seventeen parks with designated bike courses, the following have proven most popular. Rail trails are indicated with an asterisk.

Northeast

Lehigh Gorge State Park*
R.R. 2, Box 56
Weatherly, PA 18255-9512
717-443-0444

Known as a prime whitewater rafting spot, the Lehigh Gorge is equally popular with mountain bikers traversing the 25 miles between White Haven and Jim Thorpe. The unpaved bikeway follows the grade of the abandoned railroad bed of the Central Railroad of New Jersey, which used the line to haul coal from the Hazleton and Wilkes-Barre fields. There are spectacular views of rapids, waterfalls, and paddle-sport enthusiasts playing in the currents.

Southeast

Delaware Canal State Park
Box 615A, R.R. 1
Upper Black Eddy, PA 18972
610-982-5560

Delaware Canal State Park, in Bucks County, rests on the Pennsylvania/New Jersey border. The only persisting continuously intact fragment of the canal era of the early and mid-eighteenth century, the waterway transported thirty-three million tons of anthracite and six million tons of cargo during its heyday.

Today visitors can ride on a canal boat at New Hope or ride and hike the 60-mile unpaved towpath from Bristol to Easton.

Nockamixon State Park
152 Mountain View Drive
Quakertown, PA 18951
215-538-2151

Nockamixon's pride is its 1,450-acre lake set in 5,253 acres of forest in upper Bucks County. Fishing, boating, and the large swimming pool complex attract many visitors, and the 2.8-mile paved bike trail is a popular option for cyclists.

Ridley Creek State Park
Sycamore Mills Road
Media, PA 19063
610-566-4800

Where can you find a historic district in a state park? Ridley Creek, in Delaware County, has been named to the National Register of Historic Places and supports the Colonial Pennsylvania Plantation, a re-creation depicting life on a Quaker farm in 1776.

The park has a 4.7-mile paved bike path, which follows Ridley Creek, twisting and turning through a wooded ravine and past old stone farmhouses and barns.

Bicycling

Tyler State Park
101 Swamp Road
Newtown, PA 18940
215-968-2021

Tyler State Park provides cyclists with a wide, paved track. The 10.5-mile path winds beside Neshaminy Creek and through historic farmlands with views of bank barns and stone houses. Trail maps with measured segment markings are available from the park office.

South Central

Pine Grove Furnace State Park
R.R. 2, Box 399B
Gardners, PA 17324
717-486-7174

Located in the heart of Michaux State Forest, Pine Grove Furnace took its name from an early iron furnace, the ruins of which survive today. Back in 1764 this furnace turned out woodstoves, cast-iron tombstones, iron kettles, wagon-wheel rims, and cannonballs. Buildings dating to the old iron community still stand, including the office and company store, the stable, the gristmill, and several residences. The ironmaster's residence functioned during the Civil War as a station on the underground railroad and now houses a Hostelling International-American Youth Hostel.

More than 3 miles of bike paths are in the park, complemented by 2.5 miles in Michaux State Forest. Starting at the iron furnace, the route follows an old railroad bed past Fuller Lake and along Mountain Creek to Laurel Lake. Portions are paved; the remainder are dirt. Bike rentals are available at the Laurel Lake boat dock.

Pennsylvania Outdoor Activity Guide

Swatara State Park
c/o Memorial Lake State Park
R.R. 1, Box 7045
Grantville, PA 17028
717-865-6470

Swatara State Park's 3-mile bike path winds along the sinuous Swatara Creek and passes through lush woodlands and rolling farmland. The surface is a combination of pavement and crushed stone.

Northwest

Oil Creek State Park
R.R. 1, Box 207
Oil City, PA 16134
814-676-5915

An interpretive park dedicated to the story of Pennsylvania's early petroleum industry, Oil Creek provides the visitor with the opportunity to study old oil boomtowns, oil-well ruins, Indian oil pits, and foundations and cemeteries of the 1860s.

Cyclists enjoy a 9.7-mile paved trail through Oil Creek Gorge. Trailheads are at both the Petroleum Center, near the park office, and at the Drake Well Museum, operated by the Pennsylvania Historical and Museum Commission; both are open from May through the end of October. Interpretive signs and photographs portray the days when oil was black gold.

Bike rentals, snacks, and soft drinks are available at the old Egbert Oil Office at the Petroleum Center. The oil office is open daily from Memorial Day to Labor Day and on weekends in spring and fall.

Presque Isle State Park
P.O. Box 8510
Erie, PA 16505
814-871-4251 or 814-838-8776 (visitors center)

A National Natural Landmark because of its diverse geology and ecology, Presque Isle is a hook-shaped peninsula that juts 11 miles into Lake Erie and forms a protective harbor barrier for the city of Erie. Its waters once sheltered Commodore Perry's fleet until he sailed to engage the British navy in the War of 1812.

The park's paved 5.8-mile bike trail provides views of Erie and the bay. It stretches from the park entrance to the Perry Monument and is shared with roller bladers and foot traffic. A pleasant cycling break is a hike into nearby lagoons to observe the wetlands, which abound with all kinds of waterfowl and native plants.

Southwest

Moraine State Park
R.R. 1, Box 212
Portersville, PA 16051
412-368-8811

Moraine State Park is a superb example of land reclaimed and regenerated from its industrial past into a haven for recreation. Once pitted and scarred with coal mines, coal strippings, and gas and oil wells, the land is now a sylvan scene that bears little resemblance to the industrial center of the past.

The park centerpiece is 3,225-acre Lake Arthur, with a paved 7-mile bicycle track tracing portions of the north shore. Beginning at the bike rental concession building and ending at the Marina Restaurant, the trail passes open fields, stands of evergreens, and deciduous forest.

Rentals for the whole family are available weekends in May and September and daily from Memorial Day through Labor Day.

Ohiopyle State Park*
P.O. Box 105
Ohiopyle, PA 15470
412-329-8591

As the purported "gateway to the Laurel Mountains," Ohiopyle State Park contains more than 14 miles of Youghiogheny River Gorge, one of the state's most popular areas for whitewater rafting, kayaking, and canoeing. Complementing its reputation as a paddle-sport mecca, the park also has shady picnic spots, miles and miles of hiking trails, and Ferncliff Peninsula, a unique natural habitat for botanical treasures and a Registered National Natural Landmark.

Cyclists are drawn to the unpaved 25-mile bike trail, which stretches from Confluence to Ohiopyle and on to Wheeler Bottom. The path follows an abandoned railroad right-of-way paralleling the river, and there are spectacular views of the rapids and the feeder streams that cascade into the Yough (say "Yok"). A popular excursion is a morning ride on the stretch between Ohiopyle and Confluence, with the reward of lunch on the porch of the River's Edge Cafe.

NATIONAL PARK TRAILS

Gettysburg National Military Park
P.O. Box 1080

Gettysburg, PA 17325
717-334-1124

Gettysburg lives in history as the turning point of the Civil War. The fighting matched Gen. George G. Mead's 97,000-man Northern army with Gen. Robert E. Lee's Confederate army of 75,000. Meade emerged victorious, but when the dead and wounded were counted, 51,000 Northern and Southern men were numbered as casualties, proving it the bloodiest conflict in American chronicles.

To understand what happened during those decisive three days of July 1863, the visitor should interact with the terrain, either by biking or hiking the trails winding through the battlefield. Luckily, there is a paved 18-mile route, which, although shared by vehicles, is appropriate for careful cyclists and will take them to all the major sites. There is a designated cyclists' parking lot on the corner of Wheatfield Road and Sedgwick Avenue. Bike rentals are available at Artillery Ridge Campground or in town.

Valley Forge National Historical Park
Valley Forge, PA 19481
610-783-1077

One of the nation's greatest monuments to the American spirit, Valley Forge commemorates the winter of 1777–78, when George Washington's army struggled to survive against hunger, disease, and the unremitting forces of nature.

Cyclists may tour two sections of the park by utilizing either the 5.3-mile multipurpose trail from the visitors center or the shorter section from Redoubt 3 to Washington's Headquarters. The main section connects to the Schuylkill Trail near the Betzwood area.

Paths are shared with walkers and may become

crowded on busy summer and holiday weekends. Maps are available at the visitors center.

REGIONAL TRAILS

Northeast

Endless Mountain Riding Trail*
Bridgewater Riding Club
P.O. Box 21
Montrose, PA 18843
717-278-1318

For mountain bikers, hikers, horseback riders, and cross-country skiers, the Endless Mountain Riding Trail dispenses 14 miles of bucolic diversion, passing a sixty-foot waterfall and an old railroad depot. The rugged trail has its western terminal near the golf course in Montrose and ends on the far side of Martins Creek, close to Alford and US 11.

O&W Road Trail*
Rail-Trail Council of Northeast Pennsylvania
P.O. Box 100
Clifford, PA 18413
717-222-3333

In Wayne and Susquehanna Counties, the O&W Road Trail traverses 6 miles of the upper Poconos with views of the Lackawanna River, Shehawken Creek, and Stillwater Cliffs and Reservoir. A multiuse path suitable for mountain bikers, the route follows the bed of an old coal-hauling railroad between Preston Township and the Delaware River.

Bicycling

Switchback Railroad Trail*
Carbon County Park and Recreation Department
625 Lentz Trail Road
Jim Thorpe, PA 18229
717-325-3669

This 15-mile loop trail crosses the valley between Pisgah Mountain in the north and Mauch Chunk Ridge in the south—dipping down into Jim Thorpe and back up the valley to Summit Hill. Built on the bed of the Switchback Railroad, the nation's second and Pennsylvania's first operating line, the trail is rugged but relatively level.

Southeast

Fairmont Park Bikeway
Fairmont Park Commission, Memorial Hall
Philadelphia, PA 19131
215-685-0000

Philadelphia's Fairmont Park Bikeway has three sections: the 8.25-mile Schuylkill River loop, running from the Museum of Art to Kelly Drive, Falls Bridge, and West River Drive; the 7.5-mile Wissahickon Creek section, which connects with the Schuylkill Trail; and the 9-mile Pennypack Park Trail. Maps are available, and there are rentals at One Boathouse Row from March through November (215-236-43591).

Schuylkill Trail* (Philadelphia to Valley Forge Bikeway)
Montgomery County City Planning Commission
Montgomery County Courthouse
Norristown, PA 19404
610-278-3736

The Schuylkill Trail starts at the Museum of Art and runs through Fairmont Park and along the Manayunk Canal Towpath. At Port Royal Avenue the trail becomes an 11.5-mile paved bikeway along the eastern shore of the Schuylkill River. There is a recently constructed, dedicated bike path along US 422 between the trail and Valley Forge National Historical Park.

Struble Trail*
Chester County Parks and Recreation Department
235 West Market Street
West Chester, PA 19382
610-344-6415

Because it is part of the Chester County Park System and parallels a stretch of the famed Brandywine Creek, the paved Struble Trail's 2.5 miles receive heavy traffic from cyclists, naturalists, and walkers. Currently, the southern trailhead is in Downington and its northern terminal in Uwchlan Township, but the county hopes to add 15.5 miles north to Honeybrook in the future.

Towpath Bike Trail*
Palmer Township Board of Supervisors
P.O. Box 3039
Palmer, PA 18043
610-253-7191

This popular 4-mile paved trail hosts 70,000 people annually—from bike commuters to children on their BMXs. The northern end is near the Eastern Area High School; its conclusion is in Riverview Park, across the Lehigh River from Hugh Moore Park and Canal Museum.

Bicycling

North Central

Allegheny National Forest
222 Liberty Street
Warren, PA 16365
814-723-5150

    Allegheny National Forest has a variety of dual-purpose ATV/mountain bike trails totaling 213 miles. Two of the most notable are the 86.8-mile North Country Trail (see Chapter 1) and the 36.7-mile Marionville Trail.

Williamsport and Lycoming Creek Bikeways*
Lycoming County Planning Commission
48 West Third Street
Lycoming County Courthouse
Williamsport, PA 17701
717-327-2230

    Williamsport has an 11-mile urban bikeway, which stretches from Montoursville in the east to the city of Williamsport in the west, connecting with the 3.3-mile Lycoming Creek Bikeway near the Memorial Avenue Bridge. Passing through Williamsport, it is routed along city streets, and cyclists must be adept at riding in vehicular traffic.

    On the shorter Lycoming Creek stretch, the track passes through a residential area, crosses the stream from which it derives its name, and ends at Heshbon Recreation Park.

South Central

Conewago Trail*
Recreation Coordinator

Lancaster County Parks and Recreation
1050 Rockford Road
Lancaster, PA 17602
717-299-8215

The 5-mile, crushed-stone Conewago Trail is a perfect microcosm of Lancaster County, with its crooked creekside meander and its alternating passage through dusky woods and fertile farmland. Its northern terminal is near Mount Gretna Road at the Lebanon-Lancaster County line, and its southern trailhead is off State 230 to the east of the Conewago Creek crossing.

Iron Horse Trail*
Bureau of Forestry
R.D. 1, Box 42A
Blain, PA 17006
717-536-3191

The 10-mile dirt and stone Iron Horse Trail loops from its southwest trailhead in Big Spring State Park to its northeastern terminal in New Germantown. The rugged trail follows the grade of the old Path Valley Railroad, north of State 174, and in the south, the Perry Lumber Company Railroad. Suitable for mountain bikes, the track has some moderate climbs through Tuscarora State Forest.

Stony Valley Railroad Grade*
Roger L. Lehman, Chief
Pennsylvania Game Commission
2001 Elmerton Avenue
Harrisburg, PA 17100-9797
717-783-7507

Bicycling

Close to the state capital of Harrisburg, Stony Valley is a wilderness, its 41,500 acres barely disturbed by the 22-mile stone path that provides cyclists with passage through the heavy forest of oak, white pine, hemlock, beech, and maple. This was not always so.

Named Saint Anthony's Wilderness by the Moravian missionaries sent in 1742 to convert the native tribes, the area boomed when coal was discovered in 1824. After the coal era, wealthy Philadelphians "took the waters" at the curative Cold Springs. Finally the lumber barons stripped the land bare of timber. When there was nothing left to take, nature healed its wounds. Currently under the protective gaze of the Pennsylvania Game Commission, the area was the first designated under the state's Wild and Scenic Rivers Program.

Northwest

Allegheny River Trail*
Franklin Area Chamber of Commerce
1256 Liberty Street, Suite 2
Franklin, PA 16323
814-432-5823

The 14-mile asphalt and rock Allegheny River Trail begins in Franklin where the Samuel Justus Recreational Trail ends. Following the segment included in the National Wild and Scenic Rivers System, the trail crosses the 1907 Belmar Railroad Bridge and passes a set of fifty petroglyphs dated to 1200–1750. Called "The Indian God Rock," the site is listed on the National Register of Historic Places. The route terminates at Kennerdell Tunnel.

Samuel Justus Recreational Trail*
Cranberry Township
P.O. Box 378
Seneca, PA 16346
814-676-8812

From Franklin to Oil City, the paved Samuel Justus Recreational Trail winds 5.8 miles through heavy forests and passes an orchard planted by Johnny Appleseed, the Pioneer Cemetery, and old iron furnaces.

Stavich Bicycle Trail*
c/o Gary Slaven
Falcon Foundry
6th and Water Streets
Lowellville, OH 44436-0301
216-536-6221

The old bed of the Youngstown–New Castle streetcar line provides the biker with a 12-mile paved interstate route running along the Mahoning River. Accessible to the disabled, the trail is appropriate for touring bikes, in-line skating, hiking, and cross-country skiing.

Southwest

Allegheny Highlands Trail*
Somerset County Rails-to-Trails Association
829 North Center Street
Somerset, PA 15501
814-445-6433

The Allegheny Highlands Trail, from Rockwood to Markelton in Somerset County, is an essential part of the trail corridor that will eventually link Pennsylvania to our

Bicycling

nation's capital. Presently 7 of the 63 miles are complete and transport the cyclist over the hills and valleys of the eastern edge of the Allegheny Plateau.

Armstrong Trail*
Armstrong County Tourist Bureau
402 East Market Street
Kittanning, PA 16201
412-548-3226

The 48-mile trail runs along the east bank of the Allegheny River from Schenley, in Armstrong County, to Upper Hillville, in Clarion County. The cinder-based trail is open for nonmotorized use.

Ghost Town Trail*
Indiana Parks
R.D. 2, Box 157-J
Indiana, PA 15701
412-463-8636

The Black Lick Valley once held thriving industrial communities made prosperous by the area's natural resources of coal, lumber, and the railroad, which took the commodities to market. The Ghost Town Trail passes the silent remains of these towns on its 12-mile journey from Nanty Glo to Dilltown in Cambria and Indiana Counties. All six sections have a different character, from the first, which passes woodlands and parallels Blacklick Creek, to the fifth, which begins at Eliza Iron Furnace and passes near the abandoned mining town of Braken.

Great Shamokin Path*
Cowanshannock Creek Watershed Association
P.O. Box 307

Pennsylvania Outdoor Activity Guide

Rural Valley, PA 16249
412-783-6692

    This 4-mile grass and cinder trail begins at Yatesboro, near Devil's Washbasin, a small lake named for the steam that rose from its surface after nearby mines discharged hot water from their turbines. The track's eastern terminal is in NuMine, close to White Lake and its adjacent wetlands. Along the way, the route parallels Cowanshannock Creek.

Lower Trail*
Rails-to-Trails of Blair County
P.O. Box 592
Hollidaysburg, PA 16648
814-832-2400

    The 11-mile, multiuse Lower (rhymes with power) Trail has its southern trailhead in Williamsburg, in Blair County, and its northern terminal in Alexandria, in Huntingdon County. The track follows the Petersburg line of the Pennsylvania Railroad along the Frankstown branch of the Juniata River. The eight-foot-wide cycling surface is layered with crushed and rolled limestone. There is an adjoining dirt path for horses.

Montour Trail*
Montour Trail Council
P.O. Box 11866
Pittsburgh, PA 15228-0866
412-831-2030

    When complete, the entire Montour Trail will stretch 55 miles, crossing fields and forest, streams and wetlands before ending at the Monongahela River. At present the trail is divided into three sections: 8 miles commencing at the Ohio River at Coraopolis; 4.5 miles from Venice to Hendersonville, in Washington County (the Cecil Segment); and 3.5 miles in McMurray, in Washington County (the Arrowhead Trail).

RESOURCES

Regional Tour Maps

Bucks County Tourist Commission, Inc.
P.O. Box 912, 152 Swamp Road
Doylestown, PA 18901
800-836-BUCK or 215-345-4552

Maps of Kintersville-Uhlerstown–Ringing Rocks loop, 26-mile New Hope–Doylestown loop, and the historical Buckingham route.

Lancaster Bicycle Club
P.O. Box 535
Lancaster, PA 17608-0535
717-396-9299

Scenic Tours of Lancaster County, a guidebook of county tours. Fee.

Lebanon Valley Tourist and Visitors Bureau
P.O. Box 329, 625 Quentin Road
Lebanon, PA 17042
717-272-8555

Lebanon County Bike Trails, a list of four routes with maps.

Pennsylvania Outdoor Activity Guide

Wellsboro Chamber of Commerce
P.O. Box 733, 114 Main Street
Wellsboro, PA 16901
717-724-1926
   Brochure outlining three tours: the Cowanesque Valley, the Lakes region of Tioga County, and the forested mountain areas around Wellsboro and Pine Creek Gorge.

Outfitters/Tour Operators

Northeast
Blue Mountain Sports & Wear
34 Susquehanna Street
Jim Thorpe, PA 18229
800-599-4421 or 717-325-4421
Mountain bike rental, repair, sales, Shuttle service. Trail maps.

Camelback Ski Area/Alpine Slide
P.O. Box 168 (Camelback Road)
Tannersville, PA 18372
717-629-1661
Mountain bike rental. Self-guided tours on ski area trails or in Big Pocono State Park. Maps available at information desk.

Pocono Whitewater Mountain Bike Tours
Pocono Whitewater & Skirmish USA
HC 2, Box 2245 (State 903)
Jim Thorpe, PA 18229
800-WHITEWATER or 717-325-3655
Guided and self-guided mountain bike day trips through

Bicycling

Lehigh River Gorge. Shuttle service. Lunches available. Reservations requested.

Whitewater Challengers Outdoor Adventure Center
P.O. Box 8 (Route 940)
White Haven, PA 18661
717-443-9532
Guided or self-guided tours through Leslie Run Falls area and along the Lehigh River Gorge. Minimum of four for guided tours. Reservations required.

Southeast
Lumberville Store Bicycle Rental Co.
Route 32, River Road
Lumberville, PA 18933
215-297-5388
Bucks County rental of all-terrain mountain bikes. Pack lunches. Maps of Delaware Barge Canal towpath and New Jersey roads.

North Central
McBeth's Cabins
P.O. Box 115
Cooksburg, PA 16217
800-331-6317
Touring bike rentals. Ten-mile Clarion River Road routing.

South Central
Lancaster Bicycle Touring, Inc.
3 Colt Ridge Lane
Strasburg, PA 17579
717-786-4492 or 717-394-8475

Pennsylvania Outdoor Activity Guide

Two- and three-day guided tours of Ephrata, Strasburg, and Lititz. Guided tours include stays at bed and breakfasts, and leaders who are familiar with area geography and heritage. Unguided multiday or daily tours with maps and routing. Day tours by advance reservation. Open April through October.

Mount Gretna Mountain Bikes, Ltd.
1111 Walnut Street
Lebanon, PA 17042
800-279-9499 or 717-273-9499
Guided and self-guided tours. Rentals, sales, repairs, maps.

Shank's Mare
1756 South Queen Street
York, PA 17403
717-846-3132
Mountain bike rentals at store and in Codorus State Park, in Hanover. In-shop clinics and trail information.

Vermont Bicycle Touring
Box 711, Monkton Road
Bristol, VT 05443
802-453-4811
Five-day or weekend Pennsylvania Dutch tours with bed and breakfast accommodations.

Southwest
Country Pedal'rs Bicycle Touring
R.D. 6, Box 249
Somerset, PA 15501
800-762-5942 or 814-445-6316

Bicycling

Shadyside Mountain Bike Rental Center
Laurel Summit Road
Ligonier, PA 15658
412-238-2050 or 412-683-9600
Summer Saturday and Sunday mountain bike and children's bike-buggy rentals. Groups of four or more weekdays by appointment. Local touring maps available.

Ohiopyle State Park
Laurel Highlands River Tours
P.O. Box 107
Ohiopyle, PA 15470
800-472-3846 or 412-329-8531
Mountain bike rentals.

Mountain Streams
P.O. Box 106
Ohiopyle, PA 15470-0106
800-245-4090
Mountain bike rentals.

Ohiopyle Trading Post
P.O. Box 94
Ohiopyle, PA 15470
412-329-1450
Mountain bike and cruiser rentals.

River Sport Outfitters
P.O. Box 95
Confluence, PA 15424
814-395-5744
Mountain bike rentals.

Pennsylvania Outdoor Activity Guide

Spoked Wheelz
P.O. Box 142
Ohiopyle Community Center
Ohiopyle, PA 15470
412-329-1820
Mid-May to end of October. Cruiser, mountain bike, children's BMX, and bike-buggy rentals. Repair.

White Water Adventurers
P.O. Box 31
Ohiopyle, PA 15470
800-WWA RAFT or 412-329-8850
Mountain bikes, cruisers, children's bikes, and bike-buggy rentals.

Wilderness Voyageurs, Inc.
P.O. Box 97
Ohiopyle, PA 15470
800-272-4141 or 412-329-5517
Mountain bikes, cruisers, children's bikes, and bike-buggy rentals.

Youghiogheny Outfitters
P.O. Box 21
Ohiopyle, PA 15470
800-967-2387 or 412-329-4549
Mountain bike rentals.

SPECIAL EVENTS

Mid-April
Battle of Gettysburg Weekend Ride
Gettysburg-Adams County Area Chamber of Commerce

33 York Street
Gettysburg, PA 17325
717-334-6274
Rides of 25 or 50 miles held in conjunction with U.S. Cycling Federation's Battle of Gettysburg Races.

Early May
Annual Mexican Metric Century
Suburban Cyclists Unlimited
P.O. Box 401
Horsham, PA 19044
Rides of 20, 35, and 63 miles.

Mid-May
Pixton Memorial Poker Ride
Pennsylvania Bike Club
800 Welsh Road
Horsham, PA 19044
Laurama Pixton, 215-646-7879

Horse Farm Tour
Hanover Cyclers
129 Baltimore Street
Hanover, PA 17331
Rides of 25, 35, and 50 miles over rolling terrain.

Freedom Valley Bike Ride
Bicycle Coalition of the Delaware Valley and Hostelling
  International-American Youth Hostels (HI-AYH)
215-BICYCLE
Support for the Philadelphia to Valley Forge Trail.

Friday nights, June, July, and August
Lehigh County Velodrome
217 Main Street
Emmaus, PA 18098
610-967-7587
Amateur and professional racing on outdoor track. Located at State 100 and US 222, Trexlertown.

Second Weekend of June
Jim Thorpe Mountain Bike Weekend
634 South Spruce Street
Lititz, PA 17543
717-626-1742
Noncompetitive trail rides and biking events at Mauch Chunk Lake Park.

Mid-June
KAMEL (Kutztown and Millersville Eastern Loop)
Harrisburg Bicycle Club
John Donoughe
1554 Locust Street
New Cumberland, PA 17070
717-774-5073

Late June
Blue and Grey Rally, Gettysburg College
Bicycling Federation of Pennsylvania and League of American Bicyclists
c/o Tom Helm
480 Saint Johns Drive
Camp Hill, PA 17011
717-975-0925

Mid-July
The Great Ride
HI-AYH, Pittsburgh Council
6300 Fifth Avenue
Pittsburgh, PA 15232
412-422-2282
Fun rides of 25 and 35 miles.

Late August
Mon Valley Century
HI-AYH, Pittsburgh Council
6300 Fifth Avenue
Pittsburgh, PA 15232
412-422-2282
Rides of 35, 65, and 100 miles.

Covered Bridge Metric Century
Lancaster Bike Club
P.O. Box 535
Lancaster, PA 17603
717-396-9299
Rides of 31 and 62 miles.

Tour de Toona
301 Union Avenue, Suite 324
Altoona 16602
814-949-7223
Stage (road) race for Pro I, II, & III women. Point series for other categories.

Pennsylvania Outdoor Activity Guide

Tour de Christiana
107 Noble Road
Christiana, PA 17509
610-593-7176
Stage race for Pro I, II, & III women. Point series for other categories.

Early September
Labor Day Century
Hanover Cyclers
129 Baltimore Street
Hanover, PA 17331
Rides of 62 and 100 miles.

Mid-September
No Baloney Century
Lebanon Valley Bike Club
c/o Jim Deaven
124 West Church Street
Annville, PA 17003
Rides of 25, 50, 75, and 100 miles over rolling terrain.

River's Edge Century
Bicycle Club of Philadelphia
P.O. Box 30235
Philadelphia, PA 19103
Rides of 31, 62, and 100 miles over flat terrain.

Brandywine Tour
Delaware Valley Bike Club
P.O. Box 274
Drexel Hill, PA 19026
Tours of 28, 50, and 100 miles over moderately hilly terrain.

Bicycling

Sid Lustig Memorial Century
Harrisburg Bicycle Club
1011 Bridge Street
New Cumberland, PA 17070

Late September
Annual Lake Nockamixon Century
Suburban Cyclists Unlimited
P. O. Box 401
Horsham, PA 19044
Rides of 20, 35, 40, 50, 62, and 100 miles from Hatboro to Horsham.

OTHER RESOURCES

Rails-to-Trails Conservancy,
 Pennsylvania Chapter
105 Locust Street
Harrisburg, PA 17101
717-238-1717

DER, Bureau of State
 Parks
P.O. Box 8551
Harrisburg, PA 17105-8551
800-63-PARKS

DER, Bureau of Forestry
P.O. Box 8552
Harrisburg, PA 17105-8552
717-783-7941

Pennsylvania Game
 Commission
2001 Elmerton Avenue
Harrisburg, PA 17100-9797
717-783-7507

Pennsylvania Department
 of Transportation
Pedestrian & Bicycle
 Coordinator
P.O. Box 2047
Harrisburg, PA 17105-2047
717-783-8444

Tours/Accommodations
HI-AYH
P.O. Box 37613
Washington, DC 20013
202-783-6161
Non-profit association promoting low-cost outdoor travel accommodations in hostels. Their *Discovery Tours* lists both national and international cycling trips.

For information relating to the eastern region of the Commonwealth, contact:
HI-AYH, Delaware Valley Council
624 South 3rd Street
Philadelphia, PA 19147
215-925-6004

In the west, contact:
HI-AYH Pittsburgh Council
6300 Fifth Avenue
Pittsburgh PA 15232
412-422-2282

National/International Associations
Adventure Cycling Association
   (formerly BIKECENTENNIAL)
P.O. Box 8308
Missoula, MT 59807
406-721-1776
   Membership organization of more than 40,000 recreational cyclists devoted to encouraging cycling travel. They have developed 20,000 miles of bike trails nationwide,

including the East Coast Trail in Pennsylvania and the Iowa to Maine section of the Northern Tier Trail.

Their trail maps are designed to fit a handlebar bag and are broken down into 40- to 50-mile segments containing information on terrain, cycle shops, food, lodging, and both human and natural history.

In addition, the association publishes *The Cyclist Yellow Pages*, a directory of bicycling resources around the world, and the magazine *Adventure Cyclist*, which is published nine times a year and contains writeups on mountain biking, travel, and cycling advice. They also sponsor tours lasting from seven days to three months.

League of American Bicyclists
(formerly League of American Wheelmen)
190 West Ostend Street, Suite 120
Baltimore, MD 21230-3755
410-539-3399

National membership cyclists organization whose primary focus is education and advocacy. It publishes a magazine, *Bicycle USA*, eight times a year with two special issues: *The Almanac*, which lists state-by-state information on clubs, events, and special advocacy issues, and *The Tour Finder*, with a listing of touring events nationally and internationally.

State Advocacy Groups
Bicycle Coalition of the Delaware Valley
P.O. Box 8194
Philadelphia, PA 19101
Publishes a newsletter six times a year.

Bicycling Federation of Pennsylvania
P.O. Box 11625
Harrisburg, PA 17108
717-975-0888
Association dedicated to education, regulation, and legislation to make cycling easier and safer. It protects cyclists' rights in the transportation arena. Publishes a newsletter, *BikeFed UPDATE*, quarterly with a calendar of cycling events.

Lehigh Valley Bicycle Riders Alliance
348 North Ninth Street
Allentown, PA 18102-3258
Publishes quarterly newsletter.

3 HORSEBACK RIDING

Whether you aspire to a leisurely ride along mountain trails or lessons in equitation, Pennsylvania has stables and equestrian training centers to gladden the heart of every horse lover.

STABLES AND TRAINING CENTERS

Facilities can be characterized either as liveries catering to area visitors with trail rides or as English-style riding academies. At stables specializing in trail rides for transients, western saddles are the order of the day; no great expertise on the part of the rider is needed—just a willing spirit and the ability to pick up a few tips on horse control from the wrangler or guide. These outfits specialize in gentle mounts who have traveled the trails so many times that they need little instruction from the rider.

Teaching stables normally do not hire horses by the day or hour. They work over a period of time with riders, beginners or advanced, to improve skills and prepare for more advanced levels. This may include competition in "saddle seat," an English style of riding used for showing Saddlebreds, Morgans, National Show Horses, Arabians, and Tennessee Walkers. Another discipline is dressage, a word derived from the French meaning "to train." Levels of dressage range from simple maneuvers suitable to the novice to Grand Prix levels, which include fancy work such as *piaffe*, or trotting in place. Other areas of application include show jumping and eventing/combined training, a test of both horse and rider in dressage, cross-country, and jumping.

ENGLISH AND WESTERN STYLE

Most casual riders are familiar with the western style of riding, with its rocking-chair saddle and prominent saddle horn. Originally developed in California and the American Southwest, the saddle was designed to help cowboys in their daily chores of roping and riding.

English-style riding differs from western in that the saddle is streamlined, with a lower back, or cantle, and a gentle front rise called the pommel. English saddles have a single girth strap; western saddles feature rim fire, or double rigging.

Bridles and bits vary too, as does the means of reining. Horses schooled in the western style are generally neck reined, which means that the rider holds the two single reins in one hand and shifts the reins from side to side to effect a turn.

The rider on an English saddle tack-controls the mount with single reins held between the little and third fingers of each hand, or double reins held with the snaffle, or upper rein, outside the curb, or lower rein, with a finger separating the two. The two reins are then gripped together under the thumbs, which face upward. Many more distinctions exist; these are just a sample.

OTHER RIDING OPTIONS

For the advanced rider, Pennsylvania offers a wide variety of hunt and polo clubs. Polo has been called the soccer of the equine world, and it is thrilling to watch its adroit players and agile ponies.

The polo field measures 300 by 160 yards, with goalposts set at each end. Each seven-minute period is called a chukker, and there are six chukkers per game with four minutes between chukkers. The action is started when the referee "bowls" the ball between the two waiting teams, which number four players each. The players endeavor to strike the ball with the mallet's side, propelling it downfield to the goal. Of course, the team with the greatest total of goals wins.

Even if your riding skill level is far from that of the players, you'll enjoy packing a tailgate picnic, heading out to the nearest polo field, and watching the fast and furious action.

HORSE AND BRIDLE TRAILS
IN STATE PARKS AND FORESTS

The well-known Horse-Shoe Trail serves both hikers and riders, winding from Valley Forge National Historic Park in the southeast and ending 130 miles to the west in the mountains north of Hershey (see Chapter 1).

Twenty-one state parks have a sum of 155.5 miles of bridle trails for adventuring; in addition, all state forest roads, as well as areas gated and signed prohibiting motorized vehicles and mountain bikes, are paths of exploration for the rider. Extensive bridle trails exist in Wyoming, Tuscarora, and Sproul State Forests.

RESOURCES

Northeast (including Poconos and Endless Mountains)
Carson's Riding Stable
R.R. 1, Box 262
Cresco, PA 18326
717-839-9841
State 611, 1 mile south of Mount Pocono. Style/western. Guided trail rides.

Deer Path Riding Stable, Inc.
HCR 1, Box 10C (Route 940)
White Haven, PA 18661
717-443-7047 or 717-646-5254
Style/western. Guided trail rides.

Endless Mountains Resort
R.R. 3
Uniondale, PA 18470
717-679-2400
Style/western. Guided trail rides by reservation.

Horseback Riding

Inn at Meadowbrook
R.R. 7, Box 7651
East Stroudsburg, PA 18301
717-629-0296
Style/western. Guided trail rides. Indoor arena.

Mountain Creek Riding Stable
R.R. 1, Box 499 (State 940)
Cresco, PA 18326
717-839-8725
Style/western. Guided trail rides.

Pocono Adventures
HC 2, Box 2010
Jim Thorpe, PA 18229
717-839-6333
Meadowside Road off State 611, 1 mile south of Mount Pocono.
Style/western. Guided mule trips.

Pocono Manor Stables
P.O. Box 985
Pocono Summit, PA 18346
717-839-0925
Guided trail rides for beginners through advanced riders over resort's 3,000 acres.

Shawnee Stables
P.O. Box 93 (River Road)
Shawnee-on-Delaware, PA 18356
717-421-9763
Style/western. Guided trail rides.

Tamiment Resort
Tamiment, PA 18371
717-588-6652
Style/western. Guided trail rides. Pony rides.

Triple W Riding Stable, Inc.
R.R. 2, Box 1543
Honesdale, PA 18431
717-226-2620, in northeastern PA 800-540-2620
Off Owego-Milford Turnpike 4.5 miles from Hawley.
Style/western. Instruction. Guided trail rides. Overnight trips.

Southeast
Ashford Farms
P.O. Box 52 (River Road)
Miquon, PA 19452
610-825-9839
Style/English. Customized private, semiprivate, or group equestrian instruction in hunt seat or dressage. Student trail rides on fifty-five acres. Two outdoor arenas. Cross-country course.

Circle K Stables
4220 Holmsburg Avenue
Philadelphia, PA 19136
215-335-9975
Style/western. Guided rides in Pennypack Park. Pony rides.

Ferguson Farm
1895 Skippack Pike
Blue Bell, PA 19422
610-272-1206

Horseback Riding

Style/English. By appointment. Private, semiprivate, or group lessons in hunt seat. Indoor and outdoor arenas.

Gateway Stables
R.D. 3, Merrybell Lane
Kennett Square, PA 19348
610-444-9928 or 610-444-1255
Style/western and English. Full-service livery. By reservation. Certified instructors and guided trail rides for riders eight years and up. Supervised pony rides for children under eight. Lighted outdoor ring. Ninety miles of maintained trails.

Haycock Stables, Inc.
1035 Old Bethlehem Road
Perkasie, PA 18944
215-257-6271
Off State 313. Style/western and English. Instruction. Guided trail rides in Nockamixon State Park. Pony rides. Indoor and outdoor rings.

Snapfinger Farm
1020 Dewees Lane
Chester Springs, PA 19425
610-326-8077
Style/English. Instruction in hunt seat and "commonsense" horsemanship. Outdoor arena.

Thorncroft Equestrian Center
190 Line Road
Malvern, PA 19355
610-644-1963
Style/English. Structured equestrian program with private

or group instruction. Therapeutic program for physically and mentally challenged. Two indoor and two outdoor arenas.

North Central
Mountain Trails Horse Center, Inc.
R.D. 2, Box 53M
Wellsboro, PA 16901
717-376-5561
Style/western. Custom outfitter. Guided and provisioned trips of varying length. Half-day and day-long rides. Ride-and-ski or ride-and-raft Pine Creek packages.

Paradise Horses
R.R. 1, Box 64
Brookville, PA 15825
814-849-8812
Style/western and Australian. Registered Quarter Horses and Paints. Custom trail rides by appointment. Rural mountainous terrain.

Pine Crest Inc.
Star Route
Clarington (off State 36, Cook Forest), PA 15828
814-752-2375
Style/western. Trail rides.

South Central
Brittany Common Horse Center
50 Griest Road
Nottingham, PA 19362
717-529-6445

Style/English. Private, semiprivate, and group instruction by appointment in dressage, cross-country, jumping, and hunt seat. Indoor arena with Perma-Turf footing.

Gunsight Ranch
R.D. 3, Box 120A
Mifflinburg, PA 17844
717-966-4771
Style/western. Trail rides, overnight pack trips, lessons.

Heritage Acres
270 Chestnut Grove Road
Dillsburg, PA 17019
717-432-2688
Style/English. Custom private or semiprivate equestrian instruction. Three outdoor arenas, heated indoor arena.

Horse Rentals
5926 Larue Street
Harrisburg, PA 17112
717-545-5006
Stables located at 7816 Fishing Creek Valley Road. Style/English and western. Trail rides Saturday and Sunday on Horse-Shoe Trail. Group rides weekdays by reservation.

Knight's Point Stables
303 Steelstown Road
Newville, PA 17241
717-776-4646
Style/English and western. Private and semiprivate instruction. Dressage and combined training. Indoor and outdoor arenas.

Lower Hopewell Farms
390 Speedwell Forde Road
Lititz, PA 17543
717-626-7258
Style/English and western. Private, semiprivate, and group instruction by appointment in saddle seat. Indoor and outdoor arenas.

National Riding Stable
610 Taneytown Road
Gettysburg, PA 17325
717-334-1288
Style/western. By reservation, two-hour minitour in Pickett's Charge area with licensed battlefield guide, or one-hour trail ride on battlefield with trailmaster.

Nobodaddy Farm
R.D. 1, Box 401 (State 743)
Palmyra, PA 17078
717-469-0783
Style/English. Semi-private instruction for beginners through advanced in basic seat equitation. Indoor and outdoor arenas.

Rocking L Stables
201 Pleasant Hall Road (off US 11)
Carlisle, PA 17013
717-243-3174
Style/English, western, Australian. Guided trail rides. Instruction. Lighted all-weather sand ring; 150 acres with jumps. Guided trips. Children's summer day camp.

Horseback Riding

Springhill Farm
973 Shenker Road
Pottstown, PA 19465
610-326-8077
Style/English. Private, semiprivate, and group lessons by appointment in dressage, eventing, cross-country, hunter seat, quadrille, and vaulting. Lighted outdoor arena, jumping field, and cross-country course.

Total Equine Learning Center
1001B School House Lane
Lewisberry, PA 17339
717-932-4305
Style/English. Structured equestrian program with private, semiprivate and group lessons. Lighted 300-by-150-foot outdoor ring and 80-by-150-foot indoor ring. Therapeutic program for physically and mentally challenged.

Venture Farms
R.D. 1
Germansville, PA 18053
610-767-8616
Style/western. Trail rides, instruction. Outdoor arena. On Blue Mountain near Appalachian Trail.

Wind Swept Farms
4448 Fairview Road
Columbia, PA 17512
717-684-3975 or 717-684-4754
Style/English and western. Private and group lessons by appointment in dressage, hunt seat, and recreational riding. Indoor and outdoor arenas.

Windy Ridge Acres
R.D. 2
Newport, PA 17074
717-567-7457
Style/western. Guided trail rides. Private and group instruction. 125 acres of trails. Outdoor and indoor arenas.

Northwest and Allegheny National Forest
Circle W Stables & Equestrian Park
HC 3, Box 14
Tionesta, PA 16353
814-755-5920
Located at Flying W Ranch. Style/English, western. Lessons in equestrian arts. Indoor riding hall. Guided trail rides. Children's pony rides.

Pinecrest Stables
Star Route Cook Forest (State 36)
Clarington, PA 15828
814-752-2375
Style/western. Guided trail rides through eight to ten miles of deep woods. State game lands. Parent-led pony rides.

Shadow Facs Farm
2160 West Welch Road
Waterford, PA 16441
814-796-6161
Style/English. Dressage, eventing and basic balance instruction. Indoor and outdoor arenas, cross-country, stadium, and hacking areas.

Horseback Riding

Wet and Wild Acres
R.D. 1, Box 50
Brookville, PA 15825
814-752-2600
Style/western. Guided trail rides. Parent-led pony rides.

Southwest
BarGee Farms
R.D. 3, Cedar Run Road
Allison Park, PA 15101
412-767-5348
Style/English. Private, semiprivate, and group instruction by appointment. Olympic indoor arena, two outdoor arenas, derby field.

Camp Allegheny
R.D. 2, Box 212
Stoystown, PA 15563
814-754-5122
Style/western. Guided trail rides from mid-August through the first week of June.

Centennial Hill Stables
R.D. 2, Box 495
Hollsopple, PA 15935
814-479-7081
Between Thomas Mills and Jerome.
Style/English and western. Beginner through experienced guided trail rides in mountains. Overnight trips. Outdoor arena.

Pennsylvania Outdoor Activity Guide

Fallen Timber Stables
552 Boston Hollow Road
Elizabeth, PA 15037
412-751-9996
Stables located at 1501 Fallen Timber Road.
Style/western. Specializes in training western pleasure and barrel-racing horses. Private and group riding lessons by appointment. Indoor arena 60 by 150 feet; outdoor arena 150 by 250 feet.

Robert O. Mayer Riding Academy, Inc.
3284 Harts Run Road
Glenshawn, PA 15116
412-767-4902
Style/English. Beginner through competition private, semi-private, and group instruction by appointment. Specializes in dressage. Outdoor and indoor arenas.

Morning Star Stables
2277 Ridge Road
Library, PA 15129
412-655-9793. South Park area
Style/English and western. Private lessons by appointment. One indoor and two outdoor arenas.

Nemacolin Woodlands Equestrian Center
P.O. Box 188, US Route 40
Farmington, PA 15437
412-329-6961, 412-329-6957 or 800-422-2736
Style/English and western. Beginner to advanced instruction plus dressage. Guided trail rides. Indoor and outdoor arenas.

Seven Springs Resort
R.D. 1
Attn. Jack Ostrow/Mountain Trails Horseback Riding
Champion, PA 15622-9900
814-352-7777, ext. 7645
Style/western. Guided trail rides.

Smith Ranch
R.D. 1, Box 120
New Enterprise, PA 16664
814-766-2504
Guided trail rides on 267-acre farm.

EQUESTRIAN EVENTS

End of March
Lancaster County Horse Farms Open House
Participating stables. Sponsored by Pennsylvania Saddlebred Horse Association. Free self-guided tour.

Mid-April to Mid-May
Pennsylvania Special Olympics for Equestrians
Thorncroft Equestrian Center
190 Line Road
Malvern, PA 19355
610-644-1963

Third Saturday in May
Radnor Hunt Steeplechase Racing for Open Space
Hunt Club
Providence Road
Malvern, PA 19355
610-388-8346
Benefits Brandywine Conservancy.

Pennsylvania Outdoor Activity Guide

Friday before Memorial Day
Devon Horse Show and Country Fair
Horse Show Grounds
Devon, PA 19333
610-964-0550

Last weekend of May
Handicapped Riders Event of the Devon Horse Show
Thorncroft Equestrian Center
190 Line Road
Malvern, PA 19355
610-644-1963

Mid-July
Pony Express Ride
Fort Armstrong Horsemen's Association
Friendship Plaza
R.D. 6, Box 279G
Kittanning, PA 16201
412-543-1100 or 412-295-3294
Sixty-mile ride covering part of original Pennsylvania horseback mail routes.

Third weekend of July
Lawrence County Charity Horse Show
R.D. 2, Box 266
Volant, PA 16156
412-533-5612
Four-day all-breed show held at Lawrence County Fairgrounds in New Castle.

Second weekend of October
Radnor Hunt Fall Three-Day Event
826 Providence Road
Malvern, PA 19355
610-644-9918

Mid to end-October (ten-day event)
Pennsylvania National Horse Show
Farm Show Complex
Harrisburg, PA 17110-9408
717-975-3677

First weekend of November
Pennsylvania Hunt Cup Races
Newark Road
Unionville, PA 19375
610-869-0557

STATE AGENCIES

Department of Environmental Resources (DER)
Bureau of State Parks
P.O. Box 8551
Harrisburg, PA 17105-8551
800-63-PARKS
State recreation guide.

DER
Bureau of Forestry
Box 8552
Harrisburg, PA 17105-8552
717-783-7941
Bridle trail maps of Wyoming, Tuscarora, and Sproul State Forests.

EQUESTRIAN FACILITIES

Crooked Creek Horse Park
Fort Armstrong Horsemen's Association
Friendship Plaza
R.D. 6, Box 279G
Kittanning, PA 16201
412-543-1100 or 412-295-3294
For owner-riders, no hires. Facility of 113 acres with access to 100-mile trail combining Armstrong Trail and FAHA tracks. Two arenas (one lighted), grass/dressage/working area, barns, and picnic pavilion.

ASSOCIATIONS

American Horse Council
1700 K Street N.W., Suite 300
Washington, DC 20006
202-296-4031
Trade association representing the total horse industry. Monitors legislation at the federal level.

Horseback Riding

American Horse Show
  Association
220 East 42nd Street,
  4th Floor
New York, NY 10017
212-972-AHSA
Grants dates to member
  shows. Show calendar
  available. Sets standards.

Horsemanship Safety
  Association, Inc.
P.O. Drawer 39
Fentress, TX 78622
512-488-2128
Educates riders and
  certifies instructors.

North American Riding
  for the Handicapped
  Association
P.O. Box 33150
Denver CO 80233
303-452-1212

North American Trail Ride
  Conference
P.O. Box 338
Sedalia, CO 80135-0338
303-688-2292

U.S. Combined Training
  Association
P.O. Box 2247
Leesburg, VA 22075-2247
703-779-0440

Pennsylvania Equine
  Council
P.O. Box 238
Noxen, PA 18636-0238
717-624-4263 or
  717-833-5949

U.S. Dressage Federation
P.O. Box 80668
Lincoln, NE 68501
402-434-8550

U.S. Equestrian Team
Pottersville Road
Gladstone, NJ 07934
908-234-1251

U.S. Polo Association
4059 Iron Works Pike
Lexington KY 40511
606-255-0593

POLO CLUBS

Bucks County Polo Club
Bucks County Horse Park
8934 Easton Road
Revere, PA 18953
215-847-8228
Lessons and horses available. Polo games, May–October, Saturdays 2:00 to 4:00 P.M. Summer horse shows.

Brandywine Polo
  Association
Dixon Stroud, Jr.
101 East Street Road
Kennett Square, PA 19348

Darlington Polo Club
Mark Powers
74 Polo Drive
East Palestine, OH 44413

Doe Run Polo Association
Richard Jones, Sr.
Route 8, Box 398
Coatesville, PA 19320

Lancaster Polo Club
Michael F. Tracy
224 Bethesda Church
  Road West
Holtwood, PA 17534

Mallet Hill Polo Club
Alfred Fortugno
Box 61
Cochranville, PA 19330

Tinicum Polo Club
Marianne Grabowski
Box 83
Upper Black Eddy, PA
  18972

Valley Forge Trojans
Valley Forge Military
  Academy
Wayne, PA 19087

West Shore Polo Club
George Hempt
205 Creek Road
Camp Hill, PA 17011

HUNT CLUB INFORMATION

The Chronicle of the Horse
P.O. Box 46
Middleburg, VA 22117
703-687-6341 or 800-877-5467
(Subscriptions only.) The magazine's yearly Hunt Roster issue, published in mid-September, lists all clubs and their masters. Although not available on newsstands, a single copy may be obtained by calling 703-687-6341 or writing to the above address.

4 PADDLE SPORTS

Equal to the intense geologic forces that shaped Pennsylvania and thrust the Appalachians upward, water carved its patient signature on the face of the land. From the dawn of time, man saw waterways as opportune thoroughfares, a means of avoiding the natural obstacles of mountain and forest. Today's canoeist, kayaker, and whitewater rafter employ many of these same courses for recreation.

River waters are rated according to the following international rating system: class I (easy), flat water or smooth flowing water, light riffles, clear passages, occasional sandbanks and curves; class II (medium), rapids of medium difficulty, regular waves, clear and open passages with moderate current; class III (moderately difficult), numerous high and irregular waves, rocks and eddies with passages that are clear but narrow; class IV (difficult), long and powerful rapids, standing waves, holes, and boiling eddies;

class V (extremely difficult), long and violent rapids that follow each other almost without interruption—river filled with obstructions, big drops, and violent currents; and class VI (extraordinarily difficult), violent whitewater navigable only by experts when water levels are favorable.

MAJOR RIVERS AND STREAMS

Looking at the state's major river systems—the Delaware, the Susquehanna, and the Ohio—you can picture three massive trees with their branches reaching up into the highlands, their trunks rooted in the Commonwealth borders.

Delaware River

The Delaware forms the state's eastern boundary with New Jersey, leaving New York near Hancock and flowing navigable its entire length to tidewater below Trenton, New Jersey.

The 73 miles between Hancock and the Delaware Water Gap have been designated a National Wild and Scenic River, a clear, free-flowing stream passing many engaging and historic spots, such as remains of a canal system and the oldest existing wire suspension bridge in the United States. Recreational opportunities are legion. (The river is close to a major metropolitan area, so crowds can be a problem on busy summer weekends.) Canoeists and tubers (who ride the river in inner tubes), in particular, find the river irresistible. Try for a midweek or off-season paddle, and you will be richly rewarded with the sights of a serene river—Canada geese splashing in the shallows of Arrow Island, or a kingfisher diving for its supper.

The Delaware has three main feeder streams in Pennsylvania. The most northerly is the Lackawaxen, which until late May or early April provides whitewater excitement in class I through III water.

Another major feeder stream, the Lehigh, has its source in the mountains of the Pocono Plateau and flows southeast to meet the Delaware near Easton. During its passage, it offers 65 miles of the best whitewater in the metropolitan northeast. The upper section, from the Francis E. Walter Dam to Jim Thorpe, is through Lehigh Gorge State Park, an area of spectacular scenery and awesome rapids.

The last major Pennsylvania river to augment the Delaware's flow is the Schuylkill, which has its headwaters in Schuylkill County and flows eastward to Philadelphia. Its upper reaches pass areas of state game lands and agrarian tracts, but farther on it rolls through highly industrialized areas, where it is harnessed in many places by low, in-channel dams.

Susquehanna River

A great river carrying 24 billion gallons of water a day from its bifurcated branches to the Chesapeake, the Susquehanna stretches 500 miles through central Pennsylvania. It has the highest average flow and the second largest drainage area of any river in the eastern United States.

The main branch begins as an overflow of Otsego Lake in New York, dips briefly into Pennsylvania near Oakland, meanders again into the Empire State, and finally re-enters Pennsylvania near Sayre, passing through the Endless Mountains and portions of coal country until it meets its sister stream at Northumberland.

The West Branch originates in Cambria County and flows eastward, growing in volume and fed by many sustaining streams, such as Pine Creek, Moshannon Creek, Loyalsock Creek, and the Juniata River.

Pine Creek is the favorite stream of many Keystoners, not only for its spectacular passage through the thousand-foot-deep gorge called the Pennsylvania "Grand Canyon," but also for its rugged scenery and clear waters.

Moshannon Creek is a popular spring whitewater run with class I and II rapids. Nicknamed the "Red Mo," its streambed unfortunately is tinted from acid runoff from abandoned coal mines.

The Loyalsock Creek in its upper reaches nine miles beyond Lopez has some hazardous class IV to VI rapids called the Haystacks, which can be run in decked boats in low water but are generally best avoided. Beyond the Haystacks, class III waters continue through Worlds End State Park, diminishing in intensity as the river seeks a lower level and more signs of civilization appear along the banks.

Swelling the Susquehanna's waters above Harrrisburg at Duncannon, the Juniata is an affable, placid stream, free from permanent dams and obstructions. Flowing from the 56-mile Frankstown Branch and the Little Juniata, which merge at Alexandria, the "Blue Juniata" is joined at Huntington by the Raystown Branch, which in itself is more than 85 miles long. Once the source of water on the old Pennsylvania Canal, the river now is known for its excellent fishing and for providing mellow canoe touring.

Ohio River

Tarrying but a short time in Pennsylvania but spreading its feeder branches throughout the entire western part of the state, the Ohio River begins at Point State Park in Pittsburgh through the convergence of its two greatest tributaries, the Allegheny and the Monongahela Rivers.

The Monongahela (known as the "Mon") is sustained by the Youghiogheny River. Affectionately dubbed the Yough (say "Yok"), the north-flowing torrent is best known as a whitewater stream, especially the section north of the falls at Ohiopyle State Park. Not all its length is laced with rapids, however; more tranquil waters abide in the stretch between Confluence and Ohiopyle and again between Connellsville and McKeesport, where it merges with the "Mon."

The Ohio's other source, the Allegheny River, originates in Pennsylvania's north central hills, flows northwest into New York, is curbed by Allegheny Reservoir's Kinzua Dam, and meanders in a southwestern course, eventually joining the Ohio in Pittsburgh. The upper reaches are attractive to whitewater enthusiasts until mid-May; the lower sections entice canoeists with a wealth of recreational opportunities.

Feeder branches of the Allegheny include French Creek, Buffalo Creek, Red Bank Creek, Mahoning Creek, Crooked Creek, and the Clarion River. These waters are generally rated class I, and all provide engaging scenery.

The Clarion River originates in McKean County and winds southwest to join the Allegheny south of Foxburg. It is best traveled in the spring or other times of high water. A singularly attractive stream, the Clarion passes through portions of Allegheny National Forest as well as three state parks: Bendigo, Clear Creek, and Cook Forest. The latter was named by *National Geographic Traveler* as one of the country's top fifty state parks.

CANOE SAFETY

Too many people embark on a river trip without considering safety or proper preparation. They rent canoes, pile in the passengers, and shove off. If a dunking is the worst they experience, they are lucky. Like any sport, paddling, especially on fast-moving water, requires coordination and dexterity, which can be achieved only through practice. Consider the following before undertaking any excursion.

• Know the river or stream. Secure maps or guides and read them carefully. If in doubt about a section, scout it first. Recognize river hazards and avoid them.

• Know how to swim.

• Wear a properly sized personal flotation device (PFD) when on the water. Pennsylvania law specifies that all boats must have one Coast Guard–approved PFD for each person on board; any craft on state park or state Fish and Boat Commission-controlled waters must have PFDs on all nonswimmers as well as children under nine years old. In waters controlled by the Army Corp of Engineers, Pittsburgh District, PFDs must be worn by every boater at all times.

• Carry at least sixty feet of rescue line, a whistle or other hailing device, a first-aid kit, and spare paddles.

• Wear appropriate clothing—wool, polypropylene fleece, or a wet suit when the water is cold. Immersion in frigid water can rapidly create hypothermia, a potentially fatal condition.

- If you capsize, keep upstream of a swamped craft to prevent being trapped between it and a natural obstacle. In rapids, float on your back with your feet pointed downstream. Do not try to stand in moving water; your feet may become wedged between rocks by a strong current.
- Plan locations for put-in and take-out. Be sure a shuttle is available at the trip's end.
- Never canoe alone.
- Notify someone of your route before you start out.

PENNSYLVANIA WHITEWATER

Whitewater is defined as water with swift currents and obstacles that create "white" water or foam. Pennsylvania whitewater that is run by commercial guided trips varies from class II to class IV, depending on water levels. Class II rapids can become class IV when the water is at flood stage; a class IV rapid can be tamed when water levels drop.

MAJOR WHITEWATER STREAMS

Youghiogheny River

Fed by mountain streams and a large reservoir, the Youghiogheny has an ample water supply all year. Huge rocks, wreathed in mountain laurel and rhododendron, line the banks. Spruce and hardwoods blanket the Laurel Mountains, which rise more than 1,300 feet above the river.

For our purposes, the Youghiogheny River can be divided into three sections. The Upper Yough runs through

Paddle Sports

Maryland and contains class V and VI rapids, suitable for only the most skilled and experienced paddlers. With class I and II rapids, the Middle Yough, from Confluence to Ohiopyle, is ideal for practicing boating skills.

With eight major class III and IV rapids, the Lower Yough is the state's most popular whitewater journey. Recovery pools following rapids make this section less intimidating than continuous whitewater. Guided raft trips on the Lower Yough run 7.5 miles from the pool below the falls at Ohiopyle State Park to Bruner Run.

Four park concessionaires operate on the Yough from April through October. The trip takes six to seven hours. When the water level is below four feet, the trip is generally executed in four-person rafts with a guide in the fore and aft boats plus guides in kayaks on "point" and "sweep." When the water level rises above four feet, eight-person rafts are commonly used, with guides in every boat.

Outfitters provide orientation and safety lectures, rafts, paddles, Coast Guard–approved PFDs, and transportation back to your car. Some even offer lunch on the river.

Private boaters (those with their own craft or those renting from outfitters) must have a launch permit, which is issued from the park office, and must use the park shuttle from the take-out point to Old Mitchell Place parking area. Daily paddler quotas are 960 persons for the park concession outfitters and 960 persons in private, unguided vessels.

Lehigh River Gorge

In the northeast, the Lehigh River has carved a 30-mile gorge, which provides whitewater excitement during heavy water periods from March through June and again from mid-September through mid-November. Summer is relegated to float trips except for the third Saturday of July and August, when special water releases from the Francis E. Walter Dam bring river depths up to spring and fall levels. Since releases are dependent on adequate rainfall, rafters should confirm as close as possible to the day they wish to go. Reservations are a must.

Five outfitters offer guided raft trips of the Lehigh. All do either the easier Upper Gorge run of 12.5 miles or the more tumultuous Lower Gorge run of 18 miles.

Lehigh River tours generally run six-person boats, although some use larger craft in periods of very high water. Guides are in the point and sweep rafts as well as accompanying kayaks. Orientation and safety lectures, Coast Guard–approved PFDs, rafts, paddles, and transportation to and from the river are provided.

Pine Creek Gorge

Pennsylvania's Grand Canyon is a 50-mile-long, 1,000-foot-deep gorge carved into the north central mountains by the flow of Pine Creek. Although not in the same class as whitewater journeys on the Yough or Lehigh, Pine Creek has Owassee and Split Rock rapids to provide the rafter with a taste of excitement. Two outfitters offer guided trips on the 20-mile section from Blackwell to Ansonia from mid-March to mid-June when water levels are high.

WHITEWATER SAFETY

All professional rafting companies use top-quality equipment and trained river guides. The four companies offering guided trips on the Youghiogheny are concessionaires of Ohiopyle State Park; regulations specify that guides must be at least eighteen years old, have had a year of whitewater boating experience with thirty days of experience as a guide (six of these days on the Yok), have completed standard first-aid, cardiopulmonary resuscitation (CPR), and senior lifesaving courses, and have been trained in safety procedures as well as park history and regulations.

Likewise, commercial rafting companies offering guided trips on the Lehigh must be licensed by Lehigh Gorge State Park and must conform to all park regulations.

SPECIAL CONDITIONS

Whitewater outfitters have a minimum age requirement, ranging from eighteen years for spring conditions on the Lehigh and Youghiogheny to seven years during normal water levels on the more gentle waters of Pine Creek. Most companies do not require trip participants to be swimmers, because rafters must wear Coast Guard–approved PFDs, which provide flotation in the event a paddler and raft part company. All outfitters agree, however, that no one with a fear of fast-moving water should attempt a trip, and they stress that potential rafters be in good physical condition. These are not passive trips.

CLOTHING

Special clothing is not a consideration during clement weather. All you need on a summer day is a swim suit worn under shorts, a hat firmly planted atop the head, unbreakable sunglasses, a long-sleeved shirt to prevent sunburn, and sunscreen. Shoes are mandatory in all seasons; river rocks can be sharp and will bruise or cut bare feet. River sandals are ideal, but an old pair of sneakers will do just fine.

In the early spring or fall, wool or polypropylene clothing, which retains body heat even when wet, is advisable; a wet suit may be necessary. Several rafting companies running the Lehigh River Gorge require wet suits through the month of April. Most outfitters offer rentals, but check before you go.

Take a change of clothing for the end of the trip. Your river gear will be wet and clammy by the time you finish.

STILL WATER

Pennsylvania has innumerable lakes, large and small, for still-water boaters. Access to these waters is controlled by individual counties or a variety of agencies, among them the Pennsylvania Fish and Boat Commission, the Pennsylvania Game Commission, the Pennsylvania Department of Environmental Resources's Bureau of State Parks and Bureau of Forestry, and the U.S. Army Corps of Engineers.

The state Fish and Boat Commission publishes a *Guide to Public Fishing Waters and Boating Access in Pennsylvania*, which is an excellent source of information on all state waters. Lakes as well as stream accesses are listed by county and include road directions, responsible agency, size in acres, ramp type, available parking, any launch charge, handicapped facilities, and the primary type of boating at the facility.

All boats launched on state park waters must possess

Paddle Sports

either a Pennsylvania registration or a launch permit obtained from the park office.

RESOURCES

National Organizations

America Outdoors
P.O. Box 1348
Knoxville, TN 37901
615-524-4814
National trade organization of outfitters. Free directory.

American Canoe Association
7432 Alban Station Boulevard, Suite B226
Springfield, VA 22150
703-451-0141
Country's largest and most active canoeing organization.

American Rivers
801 Pennsylvania Avenue SE, Suite 303
Washington, D.C. 20003
202-547-6900
Association to "preserve and restore America's river systems and to foster a rivers stewardship ethic."

American Whitewater Affiliation
P.O. Box 85
Phoenicia, NY 12464
914-688-5569
National membership organization promoting whitewater recreation, conservation, and access.

Pennsylvania Outdoor Activity Guide

National Association of Canoe Liveries & Outfitters
Box 248
Butler, KY 41006-9674
606-472-2205

National Organization for River Sports
314 North 20th Street, P.O. Box 6847
Colorado Springs, CO 80934
719-473-2466

North American Paddlesports Association
12455 North Wauwatosa Road
Mequon, WI 53092
414-242-5228
Trade association for producers, sellers, and marketers of paddle-sport products or services.

U.S. Canoe Association
606 Ross Street
Middletown, OH 45044
513-422-3739
Educational corporation dedicated to unification of paddlers through focusing on "competition, conservation, camping, cruising, and camaraderie."

State and Federal Agencies

Army Corps of Engineers
1000 Liberty Avenue
Pittsburgh, PA 15222
412-644-6872

Paddle Sports

Pennsylvania Department of Environmental Resources
Bureau of Forestry
P.O. Box 8552
Harrisburg, PA 17105-8552
717-787-2703

Pennsylvania Department of Environmental Resources
Bureau of State Parks
P.O. Box 8551
Harrisburg, PA 17105-8551
800-63-PARKS

Pennsylvania Fish and Boat Commission
Bureau of Boating
P.O. Box 6700
Harrisburg, PA 17106
717-657-4518
General information, safety regulations, pamphlets, and *Guide to Public Fishing Waters and Boating Access in Pennsylvania*.

Pennsylvania Game Commission
2001 Elmerton Avenue
Harrisburg, PA 17110-9797
717-787-4250

U.S. Army Corps of Engineers
P.O. Box 1715
Baltimore, MD 21203
410-962-7608

Pennsylvania Outdoor Activity Guide

U.S. Army Corps of Engineers
2nd and Chestnut Streets
Philadelphia, PA 19106
215-925-9380

Maps and Guides

Canoeing Streams of the Upper Ohio Basin, Thomas L. Gray, 11121 Dewey Road, Kensington, MD 20795.

Canoeing Guide to Western Pennsylvania and Northern West Virginia, American Youth Hostels, Pittsburgh Council, Publishing Committee, 6300 Fifth Avenue, Pittsburgh, PA 15232, 412-422-2282.

The Delaware, Delaware River Basin Commission, Box 7360, West Trenton, NJ 08628, 609-883-9500.

80 Miles of Wilderness Adventure on the West Branch of the Susquehanna River, Bucktail Council B.S.A., 209 First Street, DuBois, PA 15801.

Quiet Water: Canoe Guide to Pennsylvania, Linda and Scott Shalaway, AMC Books, 5 Joy Street, Boston, MA 02108, 800-262-4455.

Schuylkill River Users Guide, State Book Store, 20 South Third Street, Harrisburg, PA 17101, 717-787-5109.

Susquehanna Water Trails, Endless Mountains Tourist Bureau, R.R. 6, Box 132A, Tunkhannock, PA 18657-9232, 800-769-8999 or 717-836-5431.

Youghiogheny River Guide, American Canoe Association Book Service, P.O. Box 1190, Newington, VA 22122-1190, 703-550-7523.

Navigation/Nautical Charts

Allegheny, Monongahela, Ohio Rivers: Army Corps of Engineers, 1000 Liberty Avenue, Pittsburgh, PA 15222, 412-644-6872.

Lake Erie and Delaware River: Distribution Branch (NCG33), National Ocean Service, Riverdale, MD 20737, 301-436-6990. For Erie charts, order Nautical Chart Catalog 4; for Delaware River, order Catalog 1.

Liveries and Outfitters

Allegheny River
Allegheny Outfitters
P.O. Box 691
Warren, PA 16365
814-723-1203
Equipment rentals: canoes.

Brandywine River
Northbrook Canoe Company
Beagle Road, Northbrook
West Chester, PA 19382
215-793-2279
Equipment rentals: canoes, tubes, splashers.

Pennsylvania Outdoor Activity Guide

Clarion River
Belltown Canoe Rental
R.D. 1
Sigel, PA 15860
814-752-2561
Equipment rentals:
　canoes.

Cook Forest Canoe Livery
P.O. Box 14
Cooksburg, PA 16217
800-699-0712 or
　814-744-8094
Equipment rentals:
　canoes, kayaks, tubes.

Foxburg Livery and
　Outfitters
P.O. Box 352
Foxburg, PA 16036
412-659-3752
Equipment rentals:
　canoes.

Love's Canoe Rental
　and Sales
3 Main Street
Ridgway, PA 15853
814-776-6285
Equipment rentals:
　canoes.

Pale Whale Canoe Fleet
P.O. Box 109
Cooksburg, PA 16217
814-744-8300
Equipment rentals:
　canoes.

Pinecrest
Star Route
Clarington, PA 15828
814-752-2375
Equipment rentals:
　canoes.

Delaware River
Adventure Sports Canoe
　and Raft Trips
P.O. Box 175
Marshalls Creek, PA 18335
800-487-BOAT or
　717-233-0505
Guided trips. Equipment
　rentals: canoes, rafts.

Paddle Sports

Anglers Roost and Hunter's Rest
Two-River Junction Float Trips
HC Box 1A
Scenic Drive
Lackawaxen, PA 18435
717-685-2010
Guides available by reservation. Equipment rentals: canoes, sport canoes, rafts, tubes, rowboats. Also Lackawaxen River.

Chamberlain Canoe Rentals
Box 155
Minisink Hills, PA 18341
717-421-0180
Overnight camping. Equipment rentals: canoes, rafts, tubes.

Indian Head Canoes
R.D. 3, No. 7
Hampton Downs
Newton, NJ 07860
800-874-BOAT
Equipment rentals: canoes, rafts, kayaks, tubes. Matamoras livery.

Kittatinny Canoes
HC 67, Box 360
Dingmans Ferry, PA 18328
717-828-2338 or 800-FLOAT-KC
Guided trips. Equipment rentals: canoes, rafts, kayaks, tubes.

Lander's Delaware River Trips
R.D. 2, Box 376
Narrowsburg, NY 12764
914-252-3925
Overnight trips. Equipment rentals: canoes, rafts.

Pack Shack Adventure, Inc.
88 Broad Street, P.O. Box 127
Delaware Water Gap, PA 18327
717-424-8533 or 800-424-0955
Equipment rentals: canoes, rafts, tubes. Fully guided and provisioned trips. Also Pine Creek in spring.

Point Pleasant Canoe & Tube, Inc.
P.O. Box 6
Point Pleasant, PA 18950
215-297-8181
Equipment rentals: canoes, rafts, duckies, tubes.

Shawnee Canoe and Adventure Trips
Box 189
Shawnee-on-Delaware, PA 18356
800-SHAWNEE or 717-424-1139
Equipment rentals: canoes, rafts, tubes. Guided canoe trips. Whitewater rafting on Lehigh River.

Tri-State Canoes and Boats
Box 400, Shay Lane
Matamoras, PA 18336
717-491-4948 or 717-491-2555 or 800-56 CANOE
Equipment rentals: canoes, rowboats, rafts, tubes, one-person kayaks. Guided moonlight rafting with riverside barbecue every Saturday in July and August.

Paddle Sports

Juniata River
Millers Canoe Rental
R.D. 2, Box 13
Millerstown, PA 17062
717-589-3159
Equipment rentals: canoes and johnboats. Shuttle service on all 80 miles of river.

Lackawaxen River
Scotty's Whitewater Raft Rides and Inner Tube Float Trips
Box 646
Hawley, PA 18428
717-226-3551
Equipment rentals: rafts and tubes. Also Delaware River

Lehigh River
Jim Thorpe River Adventures, Inc.
P.O. Box 4066
Jim Thorpe, PA 18229
717-325-2570
Equipment rentals. Guided whitewater rafting.

Lehigh Rafting Rentals, Inc.
243 Main Street
White Haven, PA 18661
717-443-0604
Equipment rentals: rafts, duckies and tubes.

Pocono Whitewater & Skirmish
State 903
Jim Thorpe, PA 18229
717-325-3655
Float trips. Guided whitewater rafting.

Pennsylvania Outdoor Activity Guide

Whitewater Challengers Outdoor Adventure Center
P.O Box 8
White Haven, PA 18661
717-443-9532
Equipment rentals. Guided whitewater rafting. Kayaking clinics.

Whitewater Rafting Adventures, Inc.
P.O. Box 88
Albrightsville, PA 18210
717-722-0285
Equipment rentals: rafts and duckies. Guided whitewater rafting.

Wilderness Trekker
R.R. 1, Box 1243C
Orwigsburg, PA 17961
717-366-0165
Equipment rental: kayaks and canoes. Clinics.

Pine Creek
Canyon Cruise
R.D. 4, Box 154
Wellsboro, PA 16901
814-435-2969
Guided trips. Equipment rentals: canoes, rafts.

Pine Creek Outfitters, Inc.
R.D. 4, Box 130B
Wellsboro, PA 16901
717-724-3003

Guided trips. Equipment rentals: rafts, canoes, one- and two-person kayaks.

Pocono Lakes
Pecks Pond Rentals and Store
HC 67, Box 485
Dingmans Ferry, PA 18328
717-857-1136
Located on Pecks Pond, State 402, eight miles south of I-84, exit 8. Will transport canoes or other small boats to a variety of Pocono lakes.

Susquehanna River/West Branch
Bubb's Canoe Rentals
R.R. 2, Box 156
Hughesville, PA 17737
717-584-4547
Equipment rentals: canoes. Also Pine Creek in spring.

Tee Pee Canoe Rental at Wysox
R.D. 2, Box 138A
Towanda, PA 18848
717-265-3309
Equipment rentals: canoes.

Susquehanna River/Main Branch
Blue Mountain Outfitters
103 State Road
Marysville, PA 17053
717-957-2413
Equipment rentals: canoes, kayaks. Also Juniata River and other south central streams.

Evergreen Outdoor Center
R.D. 5, Union Deposit Road
Harrisburg, PA 17111
717-657-9476
Guided trips on Susquehanna, Lehigh, and Delaware Rivers. Equipment rentals: canoes.

Wildware Outfitters
995 Pfeiffers Lane
Harrisburg, PA 17109
717-564-8008
Equipment rentals: canoes.

Swatara Creek (Harrisburg area)
Union Canal Canoe Rental
R.D. 2, Box 605
Annville, PA 17003
717-838-9580 or 717-838-1561
Equipment rentals: canoes.

Youghiogheny River
Hazelbaker Recreational Service
R.D. 2, Box 15G
Perryopolis, PA 15473
412-736-4001
Yough from Connellsville to Sutersville. Equipment rentals: kayaks, canoes, tubes.

Laurel Highlands River Tours
P.O. Box 107
Ohiopyle, PA 15470l
800-4-RAFTIN or 412-329-8531
Guided trips on Upper and Lower Yough. Equipment rentals: rafts, canoes, duckies. Float trips.

Paddle Sports

Mountain Streams
P.O. Box 106
Ohiopyle, PA 15470
800-245-4090
Guided trips on Upper, Mid, and Lower Yough. Equipment rentals: rafts, canoes, duckies.

Ohiopyle Trading Post
P.O. Box 94
Ohiopyle, PA 15470
412-329-1450
Equipment rentals: rafts, shredders, duckies, kayaks, camping gear.

River Sport Outfitters
P.O. Box 95
Confluence, PA 15424
814-395-5744
Equipment rentals: canoes and kayaks, rafts.

Whitewater Adventurers, Inc.
Box 31
Ohiopyle, PA 15470
800-WWA-RAFT (reservations) or 412-329-8850
Guided trips on Upper, Mid, and Lower Yough. Equipment rentals: rafts, canoes, duckies, thrillseekers.

Wilderness Voyageurs, Inc.
P.O. Box 97
Ohiopyle, PA 15470
800-272-4141
Guided trips on Lower and Mid Yough. Equipment rentals: canoes, rafts, duckies. Instruction in canoe, kayak, and rock climbing.

Youghiogheny Outfitters, Inc.
P.O. Box 21
Ohiopyle, PA 15470
412-329-4549
Equipment rentals: rafts, duckies, shredders.

Note: Unguided whitewater trips on the Youghiogheny require a permit from the park office:
Ohiopyle State Park
P.O. Box 105
Ohiopyle, PA 15470
412-329-8591

5 FISHING

Living by a famous limestone creek is an education not only in the ways of nature, moving water, and the artful trout, but also in the ways of a different species, *homo piscator,* or the fisherman.

Through the winter and into early spring, the Yellow Breeches is tranquil, its waters disturbed only by the stay-at-home mallard or the patrolling muskrat. Cold snaps turn the banks into a fairyland of diamond wands when the vapor rising from the warmer steam crystallizes on icy branches.

Peace is shattered in mid-April when trout season opens. Anglers stand hip to rod tip in the water, and the banks are crowded with terrestrial Izaak Waltons. You see all kinds, from the serious dry-fly fisherman with his graphite Scott rod and Hardy reel to the eight year old with his inexpensive spinning rod and can of worms. On the spring-fed tributary lake at Boiling Springs, indignant waterfowl decry the takeover of their territory by boats and canoes filled with avid anglers.

The state Fish and Boat Commission stocks heavily in April and is supplemented by the Yellow Breeches Anglers Conservation Club, which runs its own hatchery. Walking streamside after a publicized stocking is an exercise in tolerance as a caravan of pickups filled with less than sporting fishermen wait for the stocking trucks to leave so they can harvest naive cultured trout.

Balancing this less than laudatory behavior is the angler in the catch-and-release waters near Allenberry Resort. Selecting from an assortment of barbless hooked artificial lures simulating the day's insect hatch, he patiently casts to pool and riffle. At the strike, he carefully brings the fish to net, immediately removing the lure and resuscitating the fish by moving it back and forth through the water to bring needed oxygen to its gills.

The Yellow Breeches has not only the prestige of a well-known trout stream but also the reputation of ready accessibility in terms of bordering roads and well-advantaged towns and villages supplying hearty Penn Dutch food, a warm, dry bed, and access to bait and tackle stores. In addition, in its most popular stretches it is an expansive stream where the wading angler can manifest a respectable cast without becoming hopelessly entangled in dense shoreline foliage.

Technically not a spring creek, the Breeches is generally designated a limestone stream because the soil and bedrock over which it flows are heavily laced with lime deposits, and several limestone springs feed it. With its origins high in Michaux State Forest, the Breeches gathers its waters from feeder streams as it descends to the wide Cumberland Valley, where it curves and recurves through woodlands, past fields, farms and homes, and around small islands before merging into the Susquehanna in New Cumberland, southwest of Harrisburg.

Unsubstantiated legend says that the stream's unusual name was bestowed upon it when troops of George Washington's Continental army stopped by its banks to wash the dust of war from their clothing. The tannin and silt of the stream stained their buff britches a dirty yellow, and using an early vernacular they named the creek the Yellow Breeches.

Although the Yellow Breeches and Pennsylvania's trout waters are perhaps best known and receive the most attention in books and magazines, there are other streams, rivers, and lakes for the angler after game fish or warmwater species. However, to begin with the most familiar, let's talk trout.

BROOKIES, RAINBOWS, BROWNIES, AND PALOMINOS

With more trout water than any state in the Northeast, Pennsylvania is synonymous with trout fishing. Out of the state's 42,000 miles of streams and rivers, 10,000 miles are clear and cold enough to support populations of this finned luminary. There's not a county in the Commonwealth, even urban Philadelphia, that does not support at least one trout stream.

If you're a fisherman, you're familiar with the names Big Spring, LeTort, Falling Springs, Penns Creek, the Yellow Breeches, and others. These are Pennsylvania's classic chalk waters, where anglers from all over the world come to fish. Rich in aquatic insects and plants, the clear waters are said to produce livelier, more vividly colored trout than those living in the freestone streams, which make up the majority of Pennsylvania waters.

The difference between the two classifications lies in stream origin and the terrain over which the creek flows. In Pennsylvania, most freestone streams begin from springs in the sandstone bedrock, which forms ridges and mountains; limestone streams flow over bedrock of calcium-rich limestone or begin as a large spring emanating from an underground source.

Lake trout and brook trout are the only true native species. With their dark olive backs and red-spotted sides, brook trout are Pennsylvania's official state fish and a close relative of the Arctic char and Dolly Varden. Through the years, the Pennsylvania Fish and Boat Commission has introduced other species to state waters: the brown, a European native first initiated in 1886; the rainbow, or steelhead as the lake-run variety are known, introduced in the 1880s from their natural range on the Pacific coast; and, in 1967, the palomino, an orange-hued hybrid of West Virginia Golden and several strains of rainbow. Every year the commission stocks about five million legal-sized trout in about 5,000 miles of cold-water streams and nearly 100 trout lakes.

More than 100 streams totaling more than 400 miles have been identified as having exceptional wild trout populations, securing them the rating as "Class A Wild Trout Waters." Although by definition a wild trout is stream-bred, the presence of a few wild trout in a stream does not justify the classification. Other factors, such as water quality, adequate aquatic life, and the condition of the streambed, are considered, as is the stream's ability to reproduce trout of sufficient size and abundance to support a long-term fishery.

Another ninety-plus streams are in the wilderness trout

stream program, which indicates that in addition to having adequate numbers of wild trout to sustain good fishing, the streams are remote and accessible by walk-in only. These are the spots most frequently elected by the angler secure in his skills and determined to avoid the masses.

WHEN ARE THEY BITING?

According to Pennsylvania Fish and Boat Commission observations over many years, optimum trout fishing conditions can be determined primarily by water temperature. Brookies feed best at 58°F; rainbows and brownies become active at 60°F.

SALMON, TOO

Once, Lake Erie's abused and polluted waters were considered too degenerate to salvage. Experts predicted the lake would die. The good news is that they were wrong. With the help of concerned conservationists and the cooperation of industry, the lake is far enough on the road to recovery to support recreational fishing. Today brown and steelhead trout coexist with coho and chinook salmon that migrate to Erie's tributary streams on their annual spawning runs, which start in autumn. Another variety, the Atlantic salmon, may be found in Raystown Lake. The season on both types stretches from mid-April to the end of February of the following year.

TROUT SEASON

Generally, trout season coincides with salmon season, with a reduced creel limit beginning the day after Labor Day.

Wild trout season is shorter, from mid-April until the day after Labor Day. As with all rules, there are numerous exceptions: streams providing fishing for all trout the entire year; waters restricting anglers to fly rods with artificial flies and streamers; areas where spinning gear and artificial lures, including spinners and spoons, may be used; catch-and-release waters; waters allowing trophy-sized trout in limited numbers during certain periods of the year; and so forth.

You can't be sure of the exact regulations unless you consult the *Summary of Fishing Regulations*, which you receive when you buy your fishing license. All anglers sixteen years and older need a license, which must be displayed on an outer garment when fishing. In addition, anyone fishing for trout or salmon, fishing in class A wild trout waters, or fishing in waters under special trout/salmon regulations must have a trout/salmon permit (stamp), available at an additional cost.

The license year runs from December 1 to December 31 of the following year. There are five types of license: resident, resident senior (sixty-five years and up), resident senior lifetime (sixty-five years and up), nonresident, and five-day tourist. Fishing licenses are available from any Fish and Boat Commission office, most county treasurers, bait and tackle shops, and sporting goods stores, as well as many variety and general stores. With 1,700 issuing agents in the state, you should have no trouble buying your license, even on Sunday.

FISH FOR FREE DAYS

The first weekend in June has been designated by the state legislature as "Fish for Free Days," as part of National

Fishing Week. No license is required during this time, but all other regulations are in effect.

ANGLING FOR GAME FISH

Pennsylvania's warmer waters harbor a bonanza of game fish. Whether you're after the spunky smallmouth bass, the muskellunge of the weedy shallows, or the toothsome walleye, there is a warm-water lake or stream to feed your fishing appetite.

Largemouth bass once inhabited only the western part of the state, but with stocking they now populate almost every lake and pond. A black to dark green fish with light sides and belly and a dark bar running along the sides, the largemouth prefers lakes rather than moving water, although it may be found in the sluggish backwaters of streams. Prime areas are Moraine State Park's Lake Arthur, Allegheny Reservoir, and Presque Isle Bay in the northwest, Lake Wallenpaupack in the northeast, and Raystown Lake in the southwest.

Smallmouth bass like flowing waters, riffle areas, and weed beds. They are gold green with darker vertical bars. Favorite smallmouth fishing spots include the Susquehanna and Juniata Rivers in the south central area, French Creek and the Upper Schuylkill in the southeast, the Delaware in the northeast, and the Upper Allegheny River in the northwest. Season for both large- and smallmouth bass runs from mid-June to mid-April of the following year.

With their dark backs, silver sides, and distinct black stripes, landlocked striped bass are school fish preferring the deep, open waters of lakes and rivers. They are mighty fighters. Introduced into the state through stocking programs, they may be found in the Susquehanna River at the Conowingo Dam, Lake Aldred, and Lake Clarke, and in concentration at Raystown Lake in Huntingdon County. Fishing is permitted all year, but the best time to go after these leviathans is spring, late summer, or fall.

Four fighting members of the pike family inhabit Pennsylvania waters: the muskellunge and tiger muskellunge, the northern pike, and the chain pickerel. Season for all members of the pike family runs from early May until March 14 of the following year.

The muskie is a solitary fish—light gray to greenish with irregular dark vertical bars. In rivers it favors slow-moving water edged with vegetation; in lakes it likes to lie in shallows or cruise the dropoffs. Originally found only in the northwestern part of the state, it now ranges throughout the Commonwealth due to stocking programs.

Some favorite muskie fishing waters include Conneaut Lake and the Pymatuning Reservoir in Crawford County and the Allegheny Reservoir (Kinzua Dam) in Warren County, both in the northwest; the Allegheny River in Armstrong County and Lake Arthur in Butler County, both in the southwest; Curwensville Lake in Clearfield County and the Clarion River Reservoir in Elk County, both in the north central area; the Susquehanna River in Dauphin County and the Juniata River and Raystown Branch, Raystown Lake in Huntingdon County, in the south central area; the North Branch of the Susquehanna River in Columbia, Lackawanna, and Montour Counties, and the Delaware River in Monroe County, in the northeast; and the Schuylkill River in Berks and Montgomery Counties and below the Fairmount Dam in Philadelphia County, in the southeast.

Fishing

Like the muskie, the northern pike's range once was confined to the northwest, and its habits are similar. It frequently can be found hiding in and around weed beds in the shallow areas of lakes. It has yellowish green sides with bean-shaped yellow spots. In the northwest, it may be found in Presque Isle Bay in Erie County and in Clear Lake in Crawford County; in the southwest in the Allegheny River, Mahoning Creek, Mahoning Creek Lake, and Red Bank Creek in Armstrong County; in the north central area in Walker Lake in Snyder County, the Allegheny Reservoir in McKean County, and the Allegheny River in Potter County; and in the south central area in Shawnee Lake in Bedford County and Meadow Grounds Lake in Fulton County.

The chain pickerel is a favorite of ice fishermen because it is easy to take through the ice. Of the three pikes, it is the most plentiful. Its original range includes the eastern two-thirds of the state. With a bronze back and brassy sides imprinted with a chainlike pattern, it cruises weed beds, shallow lake shoals, or the sluggish areas of clear streams.

Popular pickerel fishing spots include the West Branch of the Susquehanna River in Clearfield County, in the north central region; the Frankstown Branch of the Juniata River in Blair County and Wiconisco Creek in Dauphin County, in the south central region; Francis E. Walter Reservoir in Luzerne County and Bradys Lake in Monroe County, in the northeast; and Manatawney Creek in Montgomery County and Minsi Lake in Northampton County, in the southeast.

Walleye fishermen are a dedicated breed. They have to be, since a large percent of angling is done at night when the fish feed most heavily. Trolling or drifting is the preferred method. Originally found only in the western portion of the Commonwealth, the walleye has been introduced into many lakes statewide. It is yellow-olive with dark blotches over the back and large glassy or milky eyes.

Fishing season runs the same as for the pike family, and favored fishing spots include Lake Erie and French Creek in Erie County, in the northwest; the Allegheny, Ohio, and Youghiogheny Rivers and their tributaries, in the southwest; the Allegheny Reservoir in McKean County and Nessmuk Lake in Tioga County, in the north central area; portions of the Susquehanna and Juniata Rivers, in the south central area; Beltzville and Mauch Chunk Lakes in Carbon County and the North Branch of the Susquehanna River in Columbia, Luzerne, Montour, Susquehanna, Wyoming, and Northumberland Counties, in the northeast; and Lake Nockamixon in Bucks County and Tulpehocken Creek in Berks County, in the southeast.

Sauger and walleye have similar habits and belong to the same family. The sauger is found only in the Ohio River Basin and adapts itself to turbid water with greater facility than does the walleye. The season coincides with walleye and pike.

Shad are found only in rivers and large streams with access to the ocean; in Pennsylvania this means either the Delaware, Susquehanna, or Lehigh Rivers. Shad's spring upstream migration begins in early April and continues until June.

The restoration of shad in the Susquehanna is not just another fish story. In the 1700s and early 1800s, shad fisheries were an important part of the central Pennsylvania economy. However, construction of canal dams in the 1830s and the four large hydrodams in York Haven, Safe Harbor, Holtwood, and Conowingo between 1904 and 1932 cut off the shad from their ancestral spawning grounds.

Restoring shad to the Susquehanna was one of the main reasons the Fish Commission was founded in 1866. Today shad are returning to the Susquehanna due to new efforts and programs. To help the fish circumvent the dams, a cooperative of the hydroelectric companies, the Fish and Boat Commission, and the U.S. Fish and Wildlife Service gathers fish below the Conowingo Dam and transports them by truck to upstream spawning areas. As a further measure, the utilities have agreed to install dam fishways that in the future should enable the shad to return to their historic grounds.

The Fish and Boat Commission's Van Dyke Research Station, the world's only American shad hatchery, supplements the transport program by producing ten to fifteen million twenty-day-old shad fry and up to 100,000 four-month fingerlings each year, which are siphoned back into the river to swell the population. Progress has been slow, but lately there has been a heartening rise in the shad making their way from sea to Susquehanna waters.

PANFISH

When we're talking warm waters, we can't leave out the panfish, which ounce for ounce can give a child, or an adult for that matter, a lot of fishing pleasure. Crappie, rock bass, bluegill, pumpkinseed, yellow and white perch, bullhead, and channel catfish are plentiful in the state's ponds and lakes. Since most panfish are school fish, where you find one, there's likely to be more. They are easy to catch, there's no minimum size, the creel limit is a whopping fifty per day, and they make a tasty morsel if properly filleted.

FISHING BY BOAT

Whereas the classic image of the intrepid fisherman is fly rod and waders, a great many anglers find the convenience of a boat unbeatable. With a craft you are able to reach waters that because of isolation are impossible to access by foot or car.

Boat anglers should be aware of state regulations. All boats are required to be equipped with a Coast Guard–approved personal flotation device (PFD) for each person. Some lakes are limited to electric motors only; others may put limits on horsepower or forbid motorized craft entirely. All motorboats, including those with electric motors, are required to be registered with the Pennsylvania Fish and Boat Commission. The registration allows the owner to leave the boat in an overnight mooring area on commission lakes. All boats, powered or not, must be registered if moored overnight at a commission access area or lake. State parks will accept this registration in lieu of their launch permit.

You may buy your boat registration at all those locations selling fishing licenses. At the time of purchase you will receive *Summary of Boating Regulations*, which will aid you in understanding state directives.

STATE FISH CULTURE STATIONS

The Pennsylvania Fish and Boat Commission operates thirteen hatcheries. The seven starred have visitors centers

Fishing

open from 8:00 A.M. to 4:00 P.M. daily (groups need advance reservations). Warm-water species include largemouth bass, smallmouth bass, crappies, panfish, and channel catfish. Cool-water species are walleye, sauger, saugeye, northern pike, muskellunge, tiger muskellunge, chain pickerel, and striped bass. Cold-water species are brown, brook, rainbow, steelhead, and lake trout, and Atlantic salmon.

	Species raised
Bellefonte* (Centre County) 1150 Spring Creek Road Bellefonte, PA 16823 814-355-3371	Cold water
Benner Spring Research Station (Centre County) 1225 Shiloh Road State College, PA 16801 814-355-4837	Cold and cool water
Big Spring (Cumberland County) 844 Big Spring Road Newville, PA 17241 717-776-3170	Cold water
Corry* (Erie County) 13363 West Smith Street Extension Corry, PA 16407 814-664-2122	Cold water

Pennsylvania Outdoor Activity Guide

	Species raised
Fairview (Erie County) P.O. Box 531 Fairview, PA 16415 814-474-1514	Cold water
Huntsdale* (Cumberland County) 195 Lebo Road Carlisle, PA 17013 717-486-3419	Cold and cool water
Linesville* (Crawford County) Pymatuning Reservoir Box 127 Linesville, PA 16424 814-683-4451	Warm, cool, and cold water
Oswayo (Potter County) R.D. 2, Box 84 Coudersport, PA 16915 814-698-2102	Cold water
Pleasant Gap* (Centre County) 450 Robinson Lane Bellefonte, PA 16823 814-359-5132	Cold water
Pleasant Mount (Wayne County) P.O. Box 3 Pleasant Mount, PA 18453 717-448-2101	Cool and cold water

Fishing

Reynoldsdale* (Bedford County)
R. D. 1, Box 50
New Paris, PA 15554
814-839-2211

Species raised
Cold water

Tionesta* (Forest County)
State 2, Box 1
Tionesta, PA 16353
814-755-3524

Cold and cool water

Union City (Erie County)
13363 West Smith Street Extension
Corry, PA 16407
814-664-2122

Cool and warm water

U.S. FISH AND WILDLIFE SERVICE

Allegheny National Fish Hatchery
R.D. 1, Box 1050
Warren, PA 16365
814-726-0890
Located below Kinzua Dam. Specializing in lake trout. Open Monday to Friday, 7:30 A.M. to 4:00 P.M.

Northeast Fishery Center (Centre County)
P.O. Box 75
Lamar, PA 16848
717-726-4247
Hatchery specializing in endangered species such as the Atlantic sturgeon and Atlantic salmon. Open Monday to Friday, 7:30 A.M. to 4:00 P.M.

Research and Development Laboratory
National Biological Survey
R.D. 4, Box 63 (off US 6)
Wellsboro, PA 16901
717-724-3322
Laboratory concerned with fish ecology, culture, nutrition and health. Not a hatchery. Open Monday to Friday, 8:30 A.M. to 3:30 P.M. Self-guided tour.

FEE FISHING

Fee fishing entails paying a commercial establishment for the privilege of fishing their private stock. A state license is not required.

Northeast
Big Brown Fish and Pay Lake
State 115
Effort, PA 18330
610-681-6660 or 717-629-0427
Brown, brook, rainbow, golden, and tiger trout, and largemouth bass. Bait and tackle sales. Rod rental.

Cedar Hollow Farm
R.R. 2, Box 191
Laceyville, PA 18623
717-833-4155
Rainbow, brown, brook, and golden trout, largemouth and smallmouth bass, striped bass, and panfish. Bait and tackle sales. Rod rental.

Fishing

South Central
Arrowhead Springs
Route 2, Box 812
Newmanstown (Lebanon County), PA 17073
610-589-4830 or 610-589-5215
No-limit trout fishing. Bait, flies, and lures allowed. Rod rental. Tackle and bait sales.

Lake Tobias Wildlife Park
760 Tobias Road
Halifax, PA 17032
717-362-9126
Trout, bass, and bluegills.

Limestone Springs Fishing Preserve
930 Tulpehocken Road
Richland (Lebanon County), PA 17087
717-866-2461
No-limit rainbow trout fishing. Rod rental. Bait and tackle sales.

Southwest
DJ's Pay Lake
R.D. 1
Rural Valley (off State 85 between Kittanning and Indiana county line), PA 16249
412-783-6706
Rainbow, brook, and brown trout, crappies, largemouth and smallmouth bass. Bait.

Seghi's Five Lakes
R.D. 1, Box 325B
Smithfield, PA 15478
412-569-5329
Rainbow, brown, brook, and golden trout, carp, catfish, bullfin, and shovelhead. Bait and tackle shop.

GUIDE SERVICES

Northeast
Bill's Guide Service
Box 2566
Lake Ariel, PA 18436
717-698-6035 or 717-347-4484
Service specializing in Lake Wallenpaupack bass, stripers, and walleye. Ranger Bass boat, 18.5 feet.

Pecks Pond Rentals and Store
HC 67, Box 485
Dingmans Ferry, PA 18328
717-857-1136
Rents craft; refers local guides.

Tony Caps Guide Service
P.O. Box 29
Dingmans Ferry, PA 18328
717-828-8304
Delaware River, Lake Wallenpaupack, Pocono lakes. Shad, trout, bass.

Fishing

North Central
Allegheny Outdoors Guide Service
37 West Corydon Street
Bradford, PA 16701
814-368-8608
Allegheny National Forest and Allegheny State Park, NY, area. David Heflin, NY licensed guide. Boat fishing on Allegheny Reservoir (Kinzua Dam), float fishing on Allegheny River, ice fishing in winter on Allegheny Reservoir and small lakes and ponds, and trout fishing on local streams and creeks.

McConnell's Outdoor Adventures
P.O. Box 175
Waterville, PA 17776
717-753-5074
Books fishing tours anywhere in United States by matching sportsman with outfitter. Also guides fly fishermen for Pine Creek and its tributaries and the streams of Clinton County.

Wolfe's General Store and Slate Run Tackle Shop
State 414, Box 3
Slate Run, PA 17769
717-753-8551
Pine Creek area. Guide service, private lessons, hatch information.

South Central
Yellow Breeches Outfitters
P.O. Box 200, Two First Street
Boiling Springs, PA 17007
717-258-6752

Fly-fishing school, instruction, guiding on LeTort, Yellow Breeches, Big Spring, Falling Spring, and Clark Creek.

CHARTERS

Lake Erie
Tourist and Convention Bureau of Erie County
1006 State Street
Erie, PA 16501
814-454-7191
Request *Pennsylvania Lake Erie Charter Captains Association Directory.*

Raystown Lake
Trophy Guide Service
R.D. 3, Box 50
Huntingdon, PA 16652
814-627-5231
Striped bass specialty. Sparky Price, captain.

Yocum's Professional Guide Service
R.D. 1, Box 435-A
Huntingdon, PA 16652
814-643-5324
Sea Nymph Stripper boat, 17 feet. Joe Yocum, captain.

RESOURCES

Pennsylvania Fish and Boat Commission, Box 67000, Harrisburg, PA 17106, 717-657-4518:

Guide to Public Fishing Waters and Boating Access, comprehensive guide listing waters open to public fishing, boating access, Corps of Engineers impoundments, Department of Environmental Resources lakes, a master index to state lakes, and more. Fee.

Pennsylvania Angler, monthly magazine dealing with all facets of angling and "heads-up" boating ideas. By subscription.

Boat Pennsylvania, quarterly magazine with information on safety, reviews of prime boating spots, and boating tips and instruction. By subscription.

Identification Guide to Pennsylvania Fish, guidebook describing various fish found in Commonwealth waters, their markings, and habits. Covers thirty-two species, subspecies, or varieties in sixteen families. Fee.

Publications List, with prices and information on available books, wall charts, and pamphlets on everything from acid rain to the pleasures of panfishing. Reverse side provides information on the youth education program, Pennsylvania League of Angling Youth (PLAY).

Information on Non-PA Fish and Boat Commission Access

U.S. Army Corps of Engineers
2nd and Chestnut Streets
Philadelphia, PA 19106
215-925-9380
U.S. Army–controlled or –owned access area.

Pennsylvania Game Commission
2001 Elmerton Avenue
Harrisburg, PA 17110-9797
717-787-4250
Game commission–owned or –controlled access area.

Department of Environmental Resources,
 Bureau of State Parks
P.O. Box 8551
Harrisburg, PA 17105-8551
State parks– or state forests–owned or –controlled access area.

Lake Wallenpaupack
Pennsylvania Power and Light
Lake Wallenpaupack Office
P.O. Box 122
Hawley, PA 18428
717-226-3702
Information on four lakeshore campgrounds with launch areas.

Susquehanna River
Conowingo Lake/Muddy Run Recreation Park
R.D. 3, Box 730
Holtwood, PA 17532
717-284-4325
Recreation area created by Philadelphia Electric Company's Conowingo Dam. Fishermen's Park, recreation area, boat launches, Peach Bottom marina.

Fishing

Lancaster County Parks and Recreation
1050 Rockford Road
Lancaster, PA 17602
717-299-8215
Access guide to Susquehanna River from Three Mile Island to Conowingo Park. Launch sites, picnic areas, historic sites, mileage. Free by mail; free at office.

Lake Aldred
Pennsylvania Power and Light
9 New Village Road
Holtwood, PA 17532
717-284-2278
Brochure on Lake Aldred and recreation areas.
Phone for a copy of *Field Guide to Water Safety*, 12-minute tape on Susquehanna River safe boating procedures.
    Met-Ed/GPU, York Haven Power Station, 717-848-7108.
    Safe Harbor Water Power Corp., 717-872-0201.
    PP&L, Holtwood, 717-284-4101.
    Susquehanna Electric Peco Energy Company, 410-457-5011.

Special Events

Early February (one week)
Eastern Sports, Boat, Camping, Travel and Outdoor Show
Farm Show Complex
Harrisburg, PA
Reed Exhibition Company, 255 Washington Street, Newton, MA 02158, 617-964-3030. Largest show of its kind in the United States.

Pennsylvania Outdoor Activity Guide

Mid-February
Valley Forge Boat and Fishing Show
Valley Forge Convention Center
King of Prussia, PA 19406
215-337-4000
Four-day event. Show and sale of boats and fishing equipment.

End of March
Valley Forge Sports, Recreation and Outdoor Show
Valley Forge Convention Center
King of Prussia, PA 19406
215-337-4000
Four-day outdoor sports show.

Late April
Forks of the Delaware Shad Fishing Tournament
Scott Park
400 Northampton Street, Suite 509
Easton, PA 18042
215-390-SHAD (seasonal) or 215-250-7136
Tournament with cash prizes.

Last full weekend of September
Pennsylvania State Championship Fishing Tournament
Tidioute (Allegheny National Forest region), PA 16351
Contact Dan Gazalie, 90 Main Street, P.O. Box 242, Tidioute, PA 16351, 814-484-7322 after 5:00 P.M. Fishing for smallmouth bass, walleye, trout, muskie, and northern pike on the waters of Kinzua Dam, Tionesta Reservoir, Allegheny River, Brokenstraw Creek, and Conewango Creek.

6 BIRDING

Bird-watching affords year-round diversion—rewarding in city parks as well as the most remote forests or wildlife refuges. Your own backyard may host as many as fifty to a hundred species over the course of the year, permanent residents such as the black-capped chickadee and cardinal mixing with migrants such as warblers and the house wren.

Perhaps you are a dedicated birder with a life list, and you want to seek out a particular species or habitat. With 114 state parks, numerous city and county parks, vast forested lands, and a wealth of refuges and conservancies, Pennsylvania provides endless opportunities.

Some of the best bird-watching in the state is on the 1.25 million acres of state game lands, managed by the Pennsylvania Game Commission. All birds in the Commonwealth except imported species such as the English sparrow and the starling are protected by either federal or state laws. In addition to regulating the hunting of game species with an eye to a healthy bird population, the commission works with private landowners and state foresters to maintain and improve habitat.

The sheer numbers of birding locales are staggering, but among the many, a few stand out. To give you a border-to-border taste of what the Commonwealth offers, here are some of the "hot spots."

Northeast

Dorflinger-Suydam Wildlife Sanctuary
Long Ridge Road
White Mills, PA 18473
717-253-1185

In the early 1800s Christian Dorflinger emigrated from his native Alsace-Lorraine to Brooklyn, where he founded a successful business as a fine glassmaker. Ill health made him leave the city and seek the healthful climate of the Poconos, where he moved his factory and operations in 1862. Dorflinger Mills flourished from 1865 to 1921, producing glass fine enough to grace the tables of U.S. presidents from Lincoln to Wilson.

In 1980 the Dorflinger estate was dedicated to conservation and preservation by Dorothy and Frederick Suydam, Christian's grandson. The 600-acre site accommodates the original Dorflinger home, a museum housing the largest collection of Dorflinger glass in the United States, and a sanctuary containing a six-acre lake, a nature

Birding

trail, and the Wildflower Theatre, an open-air arena that is home to a summer music festival.

Bluebirds, wrens, and swallows compete for nesting space in the bluebird houses in the fields; ruffed grouse—Pennsylvania's state bird—are often seen in the white pine plantation; and a variety of native songbirds grace the multiflora roses and other plantings cultivated for wildlife habitat.

The sanctuary, which is open daily, is supported by members; visitors wishing to use the grounds are encouraged to join. The fee is minimal.

The glass museum is open Wednesday through Saturday from 10:00 A.M. to 4:00 P.M. and Sunday from 1:00 to 4:00 P.M. from May 15 through the end of October. There is an admission fee.

Grey Towers National Historic Landmark
U.S. Forest Service
P.O. Box 188
New Milford, PA 18337
717-296-6401

Grey Towers was the country estate of Gifford Pinchot, in 1898 the head of the Division of Forestry; under Theodore Roosevelt, he was chief forester of the U.S. Forest Service. Pinchot and Roosevelt collaborated to make the public aware of the preservation of natural resources; in the process they pushed the legislature into making conservation a national policy.

The Pinchot home was designed in 1885 by Richard Morris Hunt for James Pinchot, Gifford's father. The French chateauesque villa was refurbished when the younger

Pinchots established residence, adding more modern touches and blending structure and landscape through the use of numerous walkways, patios, gardens, and water areas.

Grey Towers is open from Memorial Day weekend to Labor Day weekend, daily, 10:00 A.M. to 4:00 P.M., and from Labor Day to Veterans Day weekend, daily, 1:00 to 4:00 P.M. Tours run on the hour.

Lacawac Sanctuary
R.D. 1, Box 518
Lake Ariel, PA 18436
717-689-9494

Lacawac Sanctuary in the northern Poconos is a singular place, home to what the Lacawac Sanctuary Foundation describes as the "southernmost unpolluted glacial lake in North America." Surrounded by ponds, bogs, marshes, meadows, and a mixed hardwood-conifer forest, the fifty-two-acre lake has been so carefully tended by its owners—coal baron William Connell and L. Arthur Watres—that field observers from the Academy of Natural Sciences in Philadelphia have used it as a laboratory for studying the effects of environmental changes caused by natural phenomena.

Lacawac has a mile loop path, the Maurice Broun Nature Trail, named for the first and best-known curator of Hawk Mountain Sanctuary. The Lacawac Sanctuary is open to the public daily. The woods host a variety of songbirds; if you're lucky and quiet, you may come upon wild turkey.

Those interested in further explorations, or in the diverse programs the foundation runs, may write for a calendar of events with happenings ranging from summer watercolor classes to educational lectures.

Southeast

John Heinz National Wildlife Refuge at Tinicum
Visitors Center
86th Street and Lindbergh Boulevard
Philadelphia, PA 19153
215-365-3118

One mile north of busy Philadelphia International Airport, Tinicum shelters the last vestiges of a once massive tidal marsh. As early as 1643 the Swedish, Dutch, and English diked and drained parts of the 5,700-acre Tinicum Marsh as grazing land for their livestock. As the area developed, more and more wetland was filled to accommodate the expanding city.

In 1955 a diked, nontidal area of 145 acres adjacent to Tinicum Marsh was acquired by the City of Philadelphia and dedicated as Tinicum Wildlife Preserve. To spare the remaining tidal wetlands and forestall further development, in 1972 Congress passed legislation authorizing the acquisition of an additional 1,200 acres to establish Tinicum National Environmental Center. After the death of Sen. John Heinz, a prime mover in the marsh's preservation, the refuge was renamed in his honor.

Operated by the U.S. Fish and Wildlife Service, Tinicum is a contrary mixture of some of the city's less lovely real estate cheek to jowl with waving marsh grass and twisting tidal creeks. Migratory birds such as bald eagles, peregrine falcons, Canada geese, great blue herons, black-crowned night herons, snowy and great egrets, killdeer, sandpipers, and a large variety of ducks use the marsh as a resting and feeding stop on their semiannual trips along the Atlantic flyway. Bird-watchers have tallied more than 280 species in the center, and more than 85 species nest here. Native mammals such as opossums, raccoons, and muskrats take refuge at Tinicum, and two rare amphibians—the eastern mud turtle and the red-bellied turtle—make it home.

Tinicum is open year-round from 8:30 A.M. until sunset. There is a wildlife observation platform and a boardwalk for nature study. Ten miles of trails negotiate habitats as diverse as tidal wetlands, a 245-acre impoundment, and a once-unproductive area reshaped to provide more food and better nesting sites for waterfowl. The eastern trailhead is at the visitors contact station, open from 9:00 A.M. to 4:00 P.M. daily; the western trailhead is near the parking lot off State 420. On weekends at 9:00 A.M., volunteers conduct free two- to three-hour nature walks dealing with varying aspects of the refuge.

Mill Grove
Audubon Wildlife Sanctuary
Audubon, PA 19407-7125
610-666-5593

John James Audubon is a name known not only to birders and ornithologists but to society as a whole. Artist, naturalist, and author, Audubon left a rich heritage. Born in 1785 in San Domingo (now Haiti), Audubon spent his childhood in France; he emigrated to America in 1803. His early years were spent wandering along the banks of the Schuylkill River and Perkiomen Creek, hunting, observing, collecting, and sketching.

Mill Grove is the only Audubon residence still standing.

The house was originally built in 1762 by James Morgan, who sold the property to John Penn, a descendant of Pennsylvania's founder. In 1784 Augustine Prevost bought it; five years later he sold it to Audubon's father, Jean, a French sea captain. Captain Audubon sent his son to manage the estate in 1804. Although the young Audubon lived there for just two years, it was there that he met and married his wife and began his fascination with native wildlife.

The old stone farmhouse, now the property of Montgomery County, has been transformed into a museum displaying all the artist's major published works, including the familiar prints from his *Birds of America*: the wild turkey, red-winged blackbird, cedar waxwing, yellow-shafted flicker, loon, blue jay, and house wren. Additional displays include Edward Marshall Boehm's porcelain birds and, on the third floor, a restored studio and taxidermy room depicting Audubon's working quarters when he lived at Mill Grove. The wainscoted foyer is adorned with murals by Philadelphia artist George M. Harding; the murals portray the story of Audubon's local exploits and depict bird life in a southern swamp and western prairie, and the bird rocks of the Saint Lawrence River.

Spacious grounds surround the house, creating an island of serenity in a heavily developed suburban area. There are 130 acres of fields and woods, abounding in flowering plants and more than 175 species of birds. You can pick up an illustrated map at the office that will direct you to the Green Trail, a mile-long loop providing views of the creek and the lead mine, which operated during Audubon's tenure and was the compelling reason for the captain's purchase of the property.

Mill Grove is open Tuesday to Saturday from 10:00 A.M.

to 4:00 P.M., and Sunday from 1:00 to 4:00 P.M. The grounds are open from dawn to dusk Tuesday through Sunday.

John J. Tyler Arboretum
515 Painter Road
Media, PA 19063-4424
610-566-5431
This 700-acre property has 20 miles of trails through habitats ranging from open fields to deep woodland. There's a large resident population of bluebirds.

For information on the birds of Bucks County and the places they may be seen, request the *Eco Adventure Guide* by contacting:
Bucks County Tourism Commission
152 Swamp Road
Doylestown, PA 18901-2451
800-836-BUCKS or 215-345-4552

South Central

Hawk Mountain Sanctuary Association
R.R. 2
Kempton, PA 19529-9449
610-756-6961

If you ever visit Hawk Mountain on a crisp fall day when the wind is from the northwest, you'll never forget the sight. From September's bald eagles, ospreys, and broad-winged hawks to November's red-tailed hawks and golden eagles, thousands of raptors soar over Kittatinny Ridge on their ordained migrations. Some pass high overhead;

others play to their human audience by gliding almost at head level.

The story of Hawk Mountain is the stuff of conservation legend. In the early part of the century, as today, people were drawn to the spectacular migration. They were not birders, however, but gunners intent on slaughter who witnessed the phenomenon. In 1932 photographer and naturalist Richard Pough recorded the immense carnage. A photograph of Pough and his brother at Hawk Mountain in 1932 shows the ground literally covered with the carcasses of dead birds.

Although unable to convince the National Association of Audubon Societies of the need for hawk protection, Pough's lectures and photographs impressed Rosalie Barrow Edge, energetic founder of the Emergency Conservation Committee, dedicated to fostering concern about North American wildlife. In the fall of 1933, just before the annual migration, Rosalie Edge borrowed $600 from a New York friend. From a local tombstone company she purchased a lease and option to buy 1,393 acres of mountaintop and surrounding forest land in a last-ditch effort to prevent the yearly slaughter. Her gallant efforts were the beginning of Hawk Mountain Sanctuary, the first refuge in the world to protect birds of prey.

Today Hawk Mountain Association has nearly 8,500 members in the United States and abroad and a yearly visitation of more than 70,000 people. The association is known worldwide as a leader in raptor study and conservation.

New arrivals should stop at the visitors center, where they'll find exhibits of the many raptor species, an explanation of the dynamics of migration, and a gift shop with a selection of reference books, field guides, and keepsakes.

Pennsylvania Outdoor Activity Guide

Near the center, a habitat area provides a miniature wetland with marsh, ponds, waterfalls, and native wildflowers and shrubs.

To see the soarers, cross the road and hike to the lookouts. The most popular spotting location is North Lookout, .75 mile from the entrance gate, with numerous overlooks and side trails along the way. Sturdy footwear is advised as the trail is very rocky; it's wise to remember that the promontories are buffeted by the wind and are colder than the forest paths. In addition to carrying the usual paraphernalia of spotting scopes and binoculars, many birders bring sit-upons to cushion the rocks, a thermos of a hot beverage, and an extra jacket or a windbreaker.

The Lookout Trail is part of a 4-mile sanctuary trail system that connects to the Appalachian Trail. Maps of the sanctuary display trails as well as contain raptor identification charts. Trails are open from dawn to dusk; smoking, pets, radios, and bicycles are forbidden.

For the most rewarding experience, try to visit during the week, especially in October. The sanctuary has become so widely known that fall weekends are fast reaching their carrying capacity.

The visitors center is open every day from 8:00 A.M. to 5:00 P.M. from September to November 8, and from 9:00 A.M. to 5:00 P.M. the balance of the year. There is a modest admission fee.

Middle Creek Wildlife Management Area
P.O. Box 110
Kleinfeltersville, PA 17039
717-733-1512

The first section of the 5,200-acre Middle Creek Wildlife Management Area was originally acquired in the 1930s by the Pennsylvania Game Commission with hunting license funds. Designated State Game Land 46, it was managed for small game. Many waterfowl passed over on their spring and fall annual migrations, but few stopped because the land was not suitable for feeding or resting. The farmland to the north had more potential, with its marshy ground, sluggish creek, and high water table.

These lowlands, located on the Lebanon-Lancaster County line, were purchased in the 1960s and 1970s with funds from a $70-million state bond issue. A dam was built, creating a shallow 400-acre lake. To make the reserve attractive to the public, the commission constructed a visitors center, hiking and nature trails, and fishing and boating areas.

Middle Creek is not a wilderness area. It is surrounded by the tidy farms of the Pennsylvania Dutch and attracts numerous guests from Cub Scout troops to serious birders. Weekend visitor counts during March and April migrations can total 3,000 people.

Depending on the season, a variety of wildlife can be seen and identified. The large flock of Canada geese remains year-round; mallards and wood ducks leave in the fall, returning each spring to nest. Ring-necked pheasants, bobwhite quail, songbirds, and an occasional ruffed grouse or woodcock can be spotted in the woods or along the forested fringe. Various raptors prey on the field-dwelling rodents, and in spring and summer the lake's surrounding water terraces and impoundments are home to great blue herons, little green herons, American egrets, and all varieties of wading and shorebirds.

There is a total of 12 miles of trails at Middle Creek. If time is short, be sure to check out the 1.4-mile conservation trail, a forty-five-minute ramble illustrating various tree species and habitat management practices. Or try Willow Point Trail, a level 2,500-foot path leading to an excellent spotting position on the lake. The trail is closed on Monday, Tuesday, Thursday, and Saturday from September 15 until the end of Canada goose season in January. Middle Creek is open to controlled hunting, done on a permit basis from a public drawing. The refuge's operation and maintenance are paid for entirely from the sale of hunting licenses.

The visitors center is open from 8:00 A.M. to 4:00 P.M. Tuesday through Saturday, and from noon to 5:00 P.M. Sunday, from March 1 to November 30. In the first room, interpretive displays and a push-button video illustrate Middle Creek's wide range of wildlife, from the wetland's snapping turtles to the wild turkey of the forest.

The middle room's large window wall overlooks the lake, Bluebird Trail, songbird feeders, and four-story purple martin apartment. Mounted displays of raptors, waterfowl, and native mammals line the walls.

The final section houses the information desk, a "Kids Korner" with a "please touch" box, a nest display, and several snack and soft drink dispensing machines. Here's the place to pick up a map, calendar of events, and bird list.

SUSQUEHANNA RIVER EAGLE HOT SPOTS

Bald eagles have returned to the Susquehanna River and may be seen most frequently at Conowingo Fisherman's Park below the dam in Maryland, and in Pennsylvania at Muddy Run Fisherman's Park, the Safe Harbor Dam, and where Cook's Landing Road meets the river in Fulton Township.

Northwest

Brucker Great Blue Heron Sanctuary of Thiel College
P.O. Box 362, Greenville, PA 16125
216-448-8911 (Edward Brucker)
412-588-7700 (Biology Department, Thiel College)

With more than 225 nests on this forty-five-acre site, the sanctuary has one of the largest populations of breeding great blue herons in Pennsylvania. The observation shelter is open year-round, but on-grounds walking is prohibited during nesting season. Late winter and spring are the best times to see birds, before foliage obscures the view.

Erie National Wildlife Refuge
R.D. 1 Wood Duck Lane
Guys Mills, PA 16327
814-789-3585

Contrary to popular belief, Erie National Wildlife Refuge is not on the shores of Lake Erie but some 35 miles south in Crawford County. Named for the Erie Indians, it is one of two national wildlife refuges in Pennsylvania.

The sanctuary is divided into two separate land elements. The Sugar Lake Unit is 10 miles east of Meadville on the outskirts of Guys Mills village. It contains 5,205 acres lying in a narrow valley with Woodcock Creek draining to the north and Lake Creek draining to the south.

The Seneca Unit is about 10 miles north of Sugar Lake and 4 miles southeast of Cambridge Springs. These less intensely managed 3,545 acres lie in a forested valley where Muddy Creek and Dead Creek provide wetland habitat.

More than 2,500 acres of wetlands provide feeding and

nesting grounds for a wide variety of waterfowl, raptors, and songbirds. There are confirmed sightings of more than 236 species, with nesting habitat for about 112 varieties.

Waterfowl migrations occur in March to early April and again from September to November. Canada geese, wood ducks, mallards, blue-winged teal, hooded mergansers, and black ducks swell the population to 2,500 ducks and 4,500 geese during peak days. Occasional visitors include bald eagles and osprey; common nesters are red-tailed hawks and American kestrels.

An observation blind overlooking Reitz Pond on the Boland/Ritchie Road provides excellent bird-watching and photographing, and there are nature trails varying in length from .5 to 3 miles.

Facilities are open from sunrise to sunset daily. You can obtain information leaflets and talk with personnel at the refuge headquarters/visitors center from 6:00 A.M. to 4:30 P.M. Monday through Friday. The center is located off State 198, .75 mile east of Guys Mills and 10 miles east of Meadville.

Presque Isle State Park
P.O. Box 8510
Erie, PA 16505
814-871-4251 or 814-838-8776 (visitors center)

Presque Isle is a hook-shaped peninsula, stretching 6.5 miles to the northeast and sheltering the city of Erie from Lake Erie's turbulent waters. This narrow spit of land is continually forming and re-forming through the action of wind and water. At four times in recorded history, the lake has broached the narrow neck that attaches it to the mainland. The name *presque isle* means "almost an island" in French.

Presque Isle is a favorite migratory bird stopover because it affords the shortest distance across Lake Erie as well as offering a diversity of habitats. At least 321 species of birds have been recorded here—35 listed as species of special concern.

The best time for birding at Presque Isle is late May, at the height of the spring migration. If the weather is bad and birds cannot fly across the lake, there is a veritable multitude of birds waiting to make the crossing.

Your first stop should be the visitors center, less than a mile from the park entrance. Here you can pick up a map and a bird checklist while browsing the exhibits on the unique plant and animal life of the peninsula. The center is open daily from 10:00 A.M. to 6:00 P.M.

If you want to explore the park's undeveloped area, head for the Ecological Reservation and Gull Point Sanctuary. Gull Point is located on a spit of land in the easternmost part of peninsula. Trails branch off from the far corner of Budny Beach parking lot. If you're quiet and alert you'll probably spot the common sora, least bittern, black-bellied plover, dunlin, red-breasted merganser, or common loon. Gull Point has been designated a natural area, and only minimum-impact activities such as walking and birdwatching are allowed. To protect nesting shorebirds, the shoreline is closed from April 1 through November 30.

The Ecological Reservation has paths winding through the thicket subclimax and climax forest of the interior. One of the most popular and accessible tracks is the paved Sidewalk Trail, which bisects the thickest part of the peninsula. Another path traverses a sand plain, an open grassy area popular with bluebirds. The reservation is prime songbird habitat and contributes to the park's reputation as one of the nation's birding hot spots.

Pymatuning State Park
P.O. Box 425
Jamestown, PA 16134-0425
412-932-3141

Pymatuning Visitor Center
R.D. 1, Box 8
Linesville, PA 16424
814-683-5545

Before glaciers swept across northwestern Pennsylvania, the Pymatuning was a lake. As the massive ice sheet moved across hill and valley, grinding away the land's contours, the tract was transformed into a swamp. The name of the lake, home to Paleo-Indians known as Mound Builders, is of Iroquois/Seneca origin and is believed to mean "crooked-mouthed man's dwelling place," referring to the district's prior occupation by the Erie tribe, whose queen was known for her deceptive dealings.

In 1913 the state legislature passed the Pymatuning Dam Act as water conservation and flood control for the Shenango and Beaver Rivers. After numerous delays, the lake was impounded in 1933–34, and in 1935 the Pennsylvania Game Commission leased the upper reservoir from the Department of Forests and Waters for a game refuge. Here they planted expansive fields of corn, buckwheat, and rye, which attracted Canada geese. Other birds followed: American coots, gadwalls, mallards, black and wood ducks, blue-winged teal, and yellowlegs. Bald eagles found the site attractive for nesting, and ever since the 1930s they have been the Pymatuning's stellar attractions, whether swooping over the lake for fish or perched by their nests on a small island visible from the visitors center.

The refuge's 2,500 acres of water and 1,170 acres of

land are a protected location for waterfowl during the spring and fall migrations. Peak fall populations occur around the middle of October, with about 20,000 geese in the refuge. In addition, many other species nest in the sanctuary and surrounding areas: coots, gallinules, sora and Virginia rails, mourning doves, little green herons, black-crowned night herons, and great blue herons. Raptors include bald eagles and twelve varieties of hawks, owls, and vultures.

The Pymatuning Wildlife Management Area visitors center is located on Ford Island, between the fish hatchery and the dam spillway. The center's 300 mounted wildlife specimens, exhibits, and wildlife dioramas give an overview of the native fauna. On the terrace, pay binoculars are popular with tourists for spotting feeding and nesting eagles.

The museum dispenses the Game Commission's driving tour booklet, which has essential information for birders wanting more than a casual acquaintance with the area. The 25-mile tour takes one to two hours and allows viewing of nesting sites, songbird habitat, beaver dams, and native mammals.

The center is open from March 1 to Memorial Day, Monday through Friday from 8:00 A.M. to 4 P.M., Saturday and Sunday from 9:00 A.M. to 5:00 P.M.; and Memorial Day to Labor Day, Monday through Friday from 8:00 A.M. to 4:00 P.M., Saturday from 9:00 A.M. to 8:00 P.M., and Sunday from 9:00 A.M. to 5:00 P.M. From Labor Day until closing on November 1, the schedule reverts to the March hours.

Birders should be aware that in the early sixties the Game Commission opened the management area for controlled goose hunting, and both the Sandy Lake and Conneaut Marsh areas have duck as well as goose hunting.

The season varies from year to year according to dates set by the U.S. Fish and Wildlife Service, but you can count on the period running from the first part of October until Christmas. There is no hunting on Sunday, so birders should use this day for their visits.

Southwest

Audubon Society of Western Pennsylvania
  Beechwood Farms Nature Reserve
614 Dorseyville Road
Pittsburgh, PA 15238-1618
412-963-6100

Originally part of the 400-acre Flynn farm just 8 miles northeast of Pittsburgh, Beechwood is the largest nature reserve in Allegheny County. The hilly terrain, which encompasses part of two valleys, was given to the Western Pennsylvania Conservancy in 1976 to preserve the natural topography of the region—fast disappearing in urban sprawl.

The current 134-acre preserve has a varied topography, including fields, thickets, woodlands, a pond, and two woodland streams. The 5 miles of trails, beginning behind the nature center, lead through some estimable birding territory. Red-tailed and broad-winged hawks are frequent spring and fall migratory visitors, and both green-backed and great blue herons may be spotted fishing in the manmade pond. The woodlands are rife with nesting songbirds such as the yellow-breasted chat, cedar waxwing, indigo bunting, and prairie warbler.

Beechwood's grounds are open from dawn to dusk 365 days a year. The hours for the Evans Nature Center, which houses a book and gift shop, wildlife displays, and a wildlife observation room, are Tuesday through Saturday from 9:00 A.M. to 5:00 P.M., and Sunday from 1:00 to 5:00 P.M.

Todd Sanctuary, off State 28 near Sarver in southeastern Butler County, is another facility operated by the Western Pennsylvania Audubon Society. This 160-acre preserve was named for W. E. Clyde Todd, former bird curator at the Carnegie Museum. The sanctuary's habitat of fields, woodlands, and stream-etched ravines is a favored birding spot, with more than 215 identified species.

Open daily, the sanctuary is largely undiscovered. Although its trails are well kept, it has minimal support facilities. Trail maps may be requested by writing or calling the society at Beechwood.

Moraine State Park
R.R. 1, Box 212
Portersville, PA 16051
412-368-8811

Moraine State Park—land once scarred with gas and oil wells, coal mines and strippings—represents a reclamation success story. The re-creation of the glacial lake that existed in the area more than 20,000 years ago has produced a variety of habitats supportive of a large and varied bird population. Bluebirds, meadowlarks, red-winged blackbirds, prairie warblers, yellow-breasted chats, white-eyed vireos, and field sparrows thrive in the open meadows; the woods are filled with everything from the tree-dwelling warblers to the ground-loving ruffed grouse.

Diving ducks such as northern pintails, green-winged teal, hooded mergansers, and American coot patrol the open waters of Lake Arthur. Dabblers like mallards, teal, and wood ducks are active in the shallow, protected areas.

Marshlands attract great blue herons, swamp sparrows, green-backed herons, and Virginia rails.

Choice waterfowl watching is from ice breakup until mid-April; the warbler migration peaks from mid-April through mid-May. The best time of day to view birds is very early in the morning before the fishermen make their presence known. Stop at the park office near the Pleasant Valley day-use area for a map and some advice about top birding spots. Hours are 8:00 A.M. to sunset.

RESOURCES

National Organizations

National Audubon Society
700 Broadway
New York, NY 10003
212-979-3000
Organization for persons interested in ecology, energy, and the conservation and restoration of natural resources, with emphasis on wildlife, wildlife habitats, soil, water, and forests. Publishes bimonthly *Audubon* magazine and quarterly *Audubon Field Notes*.

National Wildlife Federation
1400 16th Street N.W.
Washington, DC 20036-2266
202-797-6800
Federation seeking to educate, inspire, and assist individuals and organizations of diverse cultures to conserve wildlife and other natural resources and to protect the earth's

environment in order to achieve a peaceful, equitable, and sustainable future. Publishes bimonthly *National Wildlife* and *International Wildlife* magazines; monthly children's magazine, *Ranger Rick*; and 10-times-a-year newsletter, *EnviroAction*.

U.S. Fish and Wildlife Service
Region 5
300 Westgate Center Drive
Hadley, MA 01035-9589
413-253-8200

State Organizations

National Audubon Society
Mid-Atlantic Regional Office
1104 Fernwood Avenue, #300
Camp Hill, PA 17011
717-763-4985
For a local club contact, write or phone this office.

Pennsylvania Game Commission
2001 Elmerton Avenue
Harrisburg, PA 17110-9797
717-783-7507

Pennsylvania Wildlife Federation
    (affiliated with National Wildlife Federation)
2426 North 2nd Street
Harrisburg, PA 17110
717-232-3480

Western Pennsylvania Conservancy
316 Fourth Avenue
Pittsburgh, PA 15222
412-288-2777
Pennsylvania's largest private land conservation organization. Responsible for protecting nearly 200,000 acres of prime natural lands throughout western Pennsylvania—among them Frank Lloyd Wright's Fallingwater, and Audubon's Beechwood Farms—and for securing the land for Laurel Ridge, McConnells Mill, Moraine, Ohiopyle, and Oil Creek State Parks. Membership brings quarterly issues of *Conserve* newsletter, an annual conservation calendar, two free visits a year to Fallingwater, and free *Outing Guides* to 70 of the state's most captivating natural areas.

Bird Tours

Early Bird Nature Tours
63 South Park Avenue
Coatsville, PA 19320
610-383-1387
Tours led by veteran birders Larry Lewis and Bob Schutsky. Susquehanna River boat trips: May-October, Conejohela Flats for shorebirds, herons, egrets, and so forth. October–April, Conowingo Pond for waterfowl, loons, grebes, and bald eagles. Van tours, half or full day, of Presque Isle State Park, Tinicum Marsh, Muddy Run, Middle Creek, and Hawk Mountain.

7
BALLOONING AND GLIDING

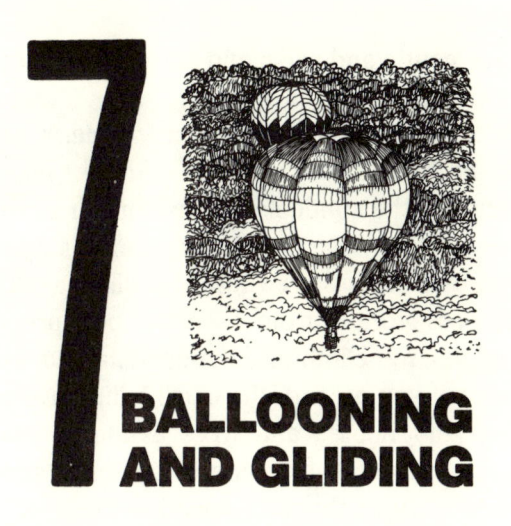

Today we travel around the globe in less time than it took our pioneer ancestors to go from Philadelphia to Pittsburgh. Acknowledging air travel as commonplace, we sacrifice the excitement of an epic age when daring aviators braved unknown worlds in experimental craft. The romance of the airways is dead, and we take solace in recreating this aura adventure through sport ballooning, sailplane soaring, or hang gliding.

HOT-AIR BALLOONS

Look up in the sky early on a calm morning or two hours before sunset. From many vantage points throughout Pennsylvania, you'll see a drop of color against the blue of the sky, a hot-air balloon drifting lazily above hill and valley, farm and field. Pilots fly at sunrise or sunset, when the winds are gentle and earth and air temperatures stabilize, eliminating pockets of turbulence.

A hot-air balloon ride is a memorable experience. Your anticipation builds at the launch site as you watch the pilot and ground crew unfold the multicolored envelope and fire the propane burners. Slowly the limp form assumes shape as more and more hot air is forced into the silken sack. When the balloon rises glorious from its earthly bed, preparations are complete. You climb into the gondola and, as the ballast is released, you ascend, the earth falling away beneath your feet and houses and trees assuming the dimensions of a doll village. The feeling of motion is suspended as you glide along at the same speed as the wind.

Almost every region of Pennsylvania has commercial licensed pilots who will sign you on for that special trip. If you want to acknowledge a friend or sweetheart with an exceptional present, the pilots also provide gift certificates. Many have special packages, and almost all celebrate the final descent with a champagne toast or its equivalent.

Balloon Tour Operators

Southeast
Balloonair
2 Sunny Hill Road
Villanova, PA 19085
610-527-1190
Weekends year-round except in winter; 45-minute flights around Chester County.

Ballooning, Inc.
76 Rock Ridge Road
Upper Black Eddy, PA 18972
610-847-2027

One-hour champagne flights near Lake Nockamixon State Park. Daily year-round.

Blue Dragon Balloons
301 East Prospect Avenue
North Wales, PA 19454
215-699-3280
Champagne and sweetheart flights.

Color the Sky
354 North Main Street
Doylestown, PA 18901
215-340-9966
FAA-certified pilot. Champagne flights, instruction. Daily year-round.

Flights Aloft
P.O. Box 63
Quakertown, PA 18951
215-536-7828
FAA-certified pilot.

Keystone State Balloon Tours, Inc.
P.O. Box 162
Pipersville, PA 18947
610-294-8034
Headquarters, Van Sant Airport, Erwinna. Champagne flights, instruction.

Lollipop Balloon
P.O. Box 523
1638 Yellow Springs Road
Chester, PA 19425
610-827-1610
Open Tuesday–Sunday, year-round.

Magical Mystery Flights
P.O. Box 622
Media, PA 19063
610-892-0860
Daily flights from West Chester. Fifth-generation balloonist and holder of 1989 state championship, 1986 tri-state championship, and several long-distance records.

U.S. Hot Air Balloon Team
P.O. Box 490, Hopewell Road
St. Peters, PA 19470
800-723-5884
FAA-certified pilots and craft. Champagne and custom flights over Lancaster or Chester Counties.

North Central
Pine Creek Hot Air Balloon Adventures
Cammal, PA 17723
717-753-8426
Weekends, by reservation only, at least one week's notice.

South Central
Adventures Aloft, Inc.
Balloon Central
P.O. Box 284
Ephrata, PA 17522
717-733-3777
One-hour flights daily year-round. Monday-Friday, full breakfast with pilot; Sunday, Continental breakfast. Central Lancaster Amish countryside.

Ballooning and Gliding

Dillon Hot Air Balloon Service, Inc.
850 Meadow Lane
Camp Hill, PA 17011
717-761-6895
Group rates for four. No flights Mondays and Fridays.

Fantasy Flights
P.O. Box 400
Center Valley, PA 18034
610-867-2229
FAA-certified pilots. Champagne flights, special packages.

Lancaster Hot Air Balloons, Inc.
P.O. Box 7776
Lancaster, PA 17604
717-560-1937
Half- and full-hour flights over Lancaster County.

Silver Lining Balloon Adventures
Harrisburg, PA
717-234-5171
Champagne flights.

Southwest
AAA Sky Ads
4967 Bakerstown Road
Tarentum, PA 15084
412-265-1310
One-hour flights over rural farmland northeast of Pittsburgh.

Pennsylvania Outdoor Activity Guide

Aerial Adventures Over Pittsburgh, Inc.
591 McCombs Road
Venetia, PA 15367
412-942-3666
One-hour champagne flights over the hills of Washington County.

Ragge & Willow Enterprises, Inc.
R.D. 7, Box 379B (US 30 east)
Greensburg, PA 15601
412-836-4777
FAA- and CAA-licensed pilots and flight instructors. Champagne flights, bed and breakfast and ballooning, sweetheart flights, fall color tours, winter wonder flights, and other packages.

Windswept Adventures
R.D. 1, Box 331-O
Ligonier, PA 15658
412-238-2555
Departs from Ligonier Valley or foothills of the Laurel Mountains, depending on wind.

State Associations

Great Eastern Balloon Association
1049 North Sekol Road, P.O. Box 635
Scranton, PA 18504
717-344-1221 or 215-322-8097
201 pilots.

John Wise Balloon Society
2111 New Danville Pike
Lancaster, PA 17603
717-872-2159
45 pilots.

National Associations

Balloon Federation of America
P.O. Box, 400
Indianola, IA 50125
515-961-8809
Supervises and documents official ballooning competitions and records attempts.

Sport Balloon Society of the United States of America
Menlo Oaks Balloon Field
P.O. Box 2247
Menlo Park, CA 94026-2247
415-326-7679
Promotes and sanctions rallies, races, and other events.

Special Events

Memorial Day Weekend
Balloon Quest
1906 Wilmington Road
New Castle, PA 16105
412-656-1200
Scotland Meadows Park, New Castle. Hot-air balloon rally and festival. Rides.

June/Father's Day weekend
Thurston Classic
Attn. Joyce Stevens
916 Diamond Park
Medville, PA 16335
814-336-4000
BFA-sanctioned event and festival. Sites vary.

Early October weekend
Fall Pumpkin Fest Hot Air Balloon Rally
Conneaut Lake Park
Crawford County Tourist Association
969 Park Avenue
Meadville, PA 16335
800-332-2338 or 814-333-1258
Balloon launches Saturday evening and Sunday morning, tethered hot-air balloon rides, festival.

Mid-October (weekend after Columbus Day)
Shawnee Autumn Hot Air Balloon Festival
Shawnee Inn
River Road
Shawnee-on-Delaware, PA 18356
800-742-9633, ext. 1405
Tethered rides, skydiving, carnival rides, food, crafts, and more.

GLIDERS AND SAILPLANES

At the dawn of time, nature sculpted parts of Pennsylvania as if in anticipation of its role as a prime soaring spot. Intense crumpling of rock followed by uplift left continuous ridges running from northeast to southwest in an unbroken line. This ideal terrain, combined with northwest winds blowing perpendicular to the ridgeline, created a highway in the sky where the future would see sailplanes dip and soar.

More than thirty world records and numerous national records have been broken by pilots from Keystone Gliderport in Julian. The world's longest glider flight of more than 1,000 miles originated here, traveled to Knoxville, and returned with no stops. Every week pilots utilize the area's winning combination of topography and wind to fly to all points of the compass. Here, as in several other areas, certified pilots take passengers aloft for what can be the thrill of a lifetime.

When it's your time to fly, things happen quickly. The tow plane lands, and your glider must be ready to hitch up. Your pilot does the preflight check, raises the canopy, and motions you to the rear seat. The plane rocks a bit as the pilot enters the glider and closes the canopy. The ground crewman attaches the towrope to the sailplane and motions the tow pilot to take up the slack. When the rope is tight, he signals "pattern clear." The pilot responds "wing up" and acknowledges with a rudder waggle, which is mirrored by the tow plane's rudder fan. The tow plane powers up, and before you know it the sailplane starts to move. Up, up you climb until the moment when altitude is reached; the pilot pulls a knob, there is a metallic ping, and you are gliding along 2,000 feet above the earth, the only noise the rush of the wind on your wings.

The following soaring clubs marked with asterisks sometimes give introductory rides at their members' convenience. They do not operate as regular charters.

SOARING CLUBS

Southeast
Cloudniners*
P.O. Box 311
Elverson, PA 19520
610-524-0160
Morgantown Airport, State 23. Weekends all year.

Country Aviation, Inc.
P.O. Box 218
Erwinna, PA 18920
215-847-8401
Van Sant Airport, Erwinna. Daily year-round.

Philadelphia Glider Council, Inc.*
100 Gillin Road
Ambler, PA 19002
215-822-9974 or 215-643-5853
Hilltown, State 152, 4 miles south of State 113. Weekends and holidays, April-December.

Soaring Society of Princeton University*
Box 1422
Princeton, NJ 08542
201-761-4876 or 215-493-0353
Van Sant Airport, Erwinna. Weekends April–December, weekdays by prior arrangement. Lessons.

North Central
Keystone Gliderport
R.R. 1, Box 414
Julian, PA 16844
814-355-2483

Ballooning and Gliding

On State 220 9 miles south of I-80, near State College. Instruction. Daily, March–December.

South Central
Blue Mountain Aviation
5363 Mountain Road
Germansville, PA 18053
610-767-4133
Out of Flying "M" Aerodrome, along the Appalachian Trail on Blue Mountain. Daily year-round.

Mid-Atlantic Soaring
Fairfield, PA 17320
301-846-4396 or 717-642-9907

National Organizations

Soaring Society of America, Inc.
Box E
Hobbs, NM 88241-7504
505-392-1177
Promotes soaring in the U.S and sanctions contests. Membership organization maintains the Soaring Hall of Fame and supports the National Soaring Museum in Elmira, NY. Publishes *Soaring* monthly and *Technical Soaring* quarterly.

National Soaring Foundation
Hobbs Industrial Park
P.O. Box 684
Hobbs, NM 88241
505-393-7328
Organization of soaring pilots dedicated to advancing the art and science of motorless flight and the preservation of the national contest site. Seminars and instruction.

HANG GLIDING

Whether it's a launch at Ringtown or Hyner View, 1,300 feet above the West Branch of the Susquehanna River, hang-glider pilots have a place to hang out in Pennsylvania. It might belabor the obvious to state that only airheads try a "hang four" without proper instruction. It might not be as self-evident that flying sites are, for the most part, administered by Commonwealth gliding clubs, which have worked to develop and maintain sites through cooperation with local landowners and, in some cases, through securing insurance and posting bonds.

Most Pennsylvania clubs require their initiates to be rated members in the U.S. Hang Gliding Association (USHGA). The organization insures its members for $1 million in liability for accidental damage to persons and property, and they have established a five-tiered rating system for pilots: beginner, novice, intermediate, advanced, and master.

The USHGA certifies instructors and keeps a current list for student reference. Instructors receiving the basic certification may teach beginner and novice levels; those with an advanced certification can teach up to master's level.

The best way a rated pilot can find a site away from his home turf is to check the USHGA magazine, *Hang Gliding* (source follows), for a list of clubs in the area he plans to fly. Many clubs will extend guest privileges to the extent of the pilot's rating.

Because club officers change on a regular basis, USHGA's information is the most current, and you are advised to check with them. If you're particularly interested in the Hyner View site, a call to Hyner Run State Park will get you the name and phone number of the up-to-date contact for Hyner Hang Gliding, Inc., the club administering the spot. Call 717-912-0257.

National Organization

U.S. Hang Gliding Association
559 East Pikes Peak, Suite 101
P.O. Box 8300
Colorado Springs, CO 80933
719-632-8300
Membership organization seeking to explore, promote, and educate in all aspects of self-launched ultralite flight, with special emphasis on safety education and communication for enthusiasts.

The association publishes *Hang Gliding*, a monthly magazine with calendar of events, club and product news, and recent developments in the sport. In addition, it keeps a current list of instructors and club contacts.

8 SKIING

DOWNHILL AREAS

Pennsylvania's twenty-eight downhill ski areas range from gentle learners' hills to full-service resorts encompassing everything from civilized novice terrain to tough black diamond expert trails. Amenities also vary, with areas catering to day skiers as well as to ski vacationers searching not only for exemplary skiing but also fine dining, shopping, and a selection of accommodations.

With fourteen resorts, the northeast region of the state has the largest concentration of downhill ski areas, centered primarily in the Pocono Mountains. Included in this mix are major areas such as Camelback, with its extensive terrain, 100 percent snowmaking, and full-service base lodge, and Fernwood, a resort with a 225-foot vertical drop and one double chair.

In the southwest's Laurel Highlands, Hidden Valley and

Skiing

Seven Springs are two full-scale resorts extremely popular with the Pittsburgh crowd and skiers from Maryland and Ohio. A cluster of day areas in the south central counties draws from the Susquehanna River Valley as well as the major metropolitan sectors of Washington, DC, and Baltimore. Two ski areas are located in the southeast not far from Philadelphia, and both Erie and Pittsburgh have small hills.

No matter where you live in the state, a ski area is within feasible commuting distance. Where you ski depends on the time you wish to invest in travel, the services you need, and the variety of terrain you require. Check the following chart for a mountain that fits your stipulations.

Northeast

Elk Mountain
R.R. 3, Box 3328
Union Dale, PA 18470
717-679-2611
Ski school, night skiing, snowboard rental
45% most difficult, 30% more difficult, 25% easier, 95% snowmaking
Longest run: 1.75 miles, total slopes & trails: 25, vertical: 1,000 ft., mountain elevation: 2,693 ft.
chairlifts: 5 double, 1 quad
snow report: 800-233-4131

Montage
P.O. Box 3539
Scranton, PA 18505
717-969-7669

Ski school, night skiing, snowboard rental
33% most difficult, 45% more difficult, 22% easier, 100% snowmaking
Longest run: 1+ miles, total slopes & trails: 18, vertical: 1,000 ft., mountain elevation: 2,000 ft.
chairlifts: 1 quad, 3 triple, 1 double, 2 tows
snow report: 800-GOT-SNOW

Spring Mountain Ski Area
P.O. Box 42
Spring Mount, PA 19478
610-287-7900
Ski school, night skiing, snowboard rental and halfpipe
20% most difficult, 40% more difficult, 40% easier, 100% snowmaking
Longest run: 2,220 ft., total slopes & trails: 7, vertical: 420 ft., mountain elevation: 528 ft.
chairlifts: 3 double, 1 triple, 1 rope
snow report: 610-287-7900 or 610-287-7300

Alpine Mountain
State 447
Analomink, PA 18320
717-595-2150
800-233-8240
Cross country, ski school, snowboard rental
25% most difficult, 50% more difficult, 25% easier, 100% snowmaking
Longest run: 2,640 ft., total slopes & trails: 18, vertical: 500 ft., mountain elevation: 1,150 ft.
chairlifts: 1 double, 2 quad
snow report: 717-595-2150

Blue Mountain
P.O. Box 216
Palmerton, PA 18071
610-826-7700
Ski school, night skiing
32% most difficult, 37% more difficult, 31% easier, 100% snowmaking
Longest run: 5,200 ft., total slopes & trails: 19, vertical: 923 ft., mountain elevation: 1,053 ft.
chairlifts: 5 double, 1 T-bar, 1 detach
snow report: 800-235-2226

Camelback
Exit 45 on I-90
Tannersville, PA 18372
717-629-1661
Ski school, snowboard rental and halfpipe
20% most difficult, 40% more difficult, 40% easier, 100% snowmaking
Longest run: 1 mile, total slopes & trails: 31, vertical: 826 ft., mountain elevation: 2,050 ft.
chairlifts: 8 double, 2 triple, 1 quad, 1 HS detach
snow report: 800-233-8100

Fernwood
US 209 north
Bushkill, PA 18324
717-588-9500
800-233-8103
Ski school
50% more difficult, 50% easier, 100% snowmaking
Longest run: 1,500 ft., total slopes & trails: 2, vertical: 225 ft.
chairlifts: 1 double
snow report: 717-588-9500

Mount Airy Lodge
Mount Pocono, PA 18344
717-839-8811
800-441-4410 (lodge)
Cross country, ski school
42% more difficult, 58% easier, 100% snowmaking
Longest run: 2,300 ft., total slopes & trails: 7, vertical: 280 ft., mountain elevation: 1,200 ft.
chairlifts: 2 double
snow report: 717-839-8811

Mount Tone Ski Resort
Off State 247
Lake Como, PA 18437
717-798-2707
908-276-0998 (reservations)
Cross country, ski school, night skiing, snowboard rental
20% most difficult, 40% more difficult, 40% easier, 85% snowmaking
Longest run: 2,500 ft., total slopes & trails: 11, vertical: 450 ft., mountain elevation: 1,930 ft.
chairlifts: 1 m. mite, 1 triple, 1 T-bar, 2 rope
snow report: 717-798-2707

Shawnee Mountain
Exit 52 off I-80
Shawnee-on-Delaware, PA 18356
717-421-7231
800-SHAWNEE (hotel)
Ski school, night skiing, snowboard rental and halfpipe
25% most difficult, 50% more difficult, 25% easier, 100% snowmaking

Skiing

Longest run: 5,100 ft., total slopes & trails: 23, vertical: 700 ft., mountain elevation: 1,350 ft.
chairlifts: 1 triple, 8 double
snow report: 800-233-4218

Split Rock Resort
Lake Harmony, PA 18624
717-722-9111
800-255-ROCK
Cross country, ski school, snowboard rental and halfpipe
50% more difficult, 50% easier, 100% snowmaking
Longest run: 1,700 ft., total slopes & trails: 7, vertical: 250 ft., mountain elevation: 1,950 ft.
chairlifts: 1 double, 1 T-bar
snow report: 717-722-9111

Tanglwood
Lake Wallenpaupack
Tafton, PA 18464
717-226-9500
Cross country, ski school, night skiing, snowboard rental
30% most difficult, 45% more difficult, 25% easier, 100% snowmaking
Longest run: 1.25 miles, total slopes & trails: 10, vertical: 415 ft., mountain elevation: 1,750 ft.
chairlifts: 2 double, 2 T-bar, 1 rope
snow report: 717-226-9500

The Big Two—Big Boulder
P.O. Box 702
Blakeslee, PA 18610
717-722-0100
800-468-BIG2 (lodge)

Cross country, ski school, snowboard rental and halfpipe
25% most difficult, 40% more difficult, 35% easier, 100% snowmaking
Longest run: 2,900 ft., total slopes & trails: 12, vertical: 475 ft., mountain elevation: 2,175 ft.
chairlifts: 2 triple, 5 double
snow report: 717-722-0100

The Big Two—Jack Frost
P.O. Box 703
Blakeslee, PA 18610
717-443-8425
800-468-BIG2 (lodge)
Cross country, ski school, snowboard rental and halfpipe
40% most difficult, 40% more difficult, 20% easier, 100% snowmaking
Longest run: 2,700 ft., total slopes & trails: 20, vertical: 600 ft., mountain elevation: 2,000 ft.
chairlifts: 1 quad, 4 double, 2 triple
snow report: 717-443-8425

North Central

Crystal Lake
R.R. 1, Box 308
Hughesville, PA 17737
717-584-2698
Cross country, ski school, night skiing, snowboard rental
10% most difficult, 60% more difficult, 30% easier, 100% snowmaking
Longest run: 1,300 ft., total slopes & trails: 4, vertical: 250 ft., mountain elevation: 2,100 ft.
chairlifts: 1 poma, 1 rope, 1 pony
snow report: 717-584-4209

Skiing

Ski Denton
P.O. Box 367/US 6
Coudersport, PA 16915
814-435-2115
Cross country, ski school, night skiing, snowboard rental and park
33% most difficult, 32% more difficult, 35% easier, 95% snowmaking
Longest run: 1 mile, total slopes & trails: 20, vertical: 650 ft., mountain elevation: 2,885 ft.
chairlifts: 1 triple, 1 double, 2 poma, 1 handle tow
snow report: 814-435-2115

Ski Sawmill Resort
P.O. Box 5
Morris, PA 16938
800-532-7669
717-353-7731 (lodging)
Cross country, ski school, night skiing, snowboard rental
20% most difficult, 30% more difficult, 50% easier, 100% snowmaking
Longest run: 3,250 ft., total slopes & trails: 8, vertical: 515 ft., mountain elevation: 2,215 ft.
chairlifts: 1 double, 2 T-bar
snow report: 717-353-7521 or 800-532-SNOW

Tussey Mountain Ski Area
P.O. Box 559
State College, PA 16804
814-466-6810
Ski school, night skiing, snowboard rental
25% most difficult, 50% more difficult, 25% easier, 100% snowmaking

Pennsylvania Outdoor Activity Guide

Longest run: 1 mile, total slopes & trails: 7, vertical: 500 ft., mountain elevation: 1,818 ft.
chairlifts: 1 quad, 1 T-bar, 1 poma, 1 handle tow
snow report: 814-466-6810

South Central
Whitetail Resort
13805 Blairs Valley Road
Mercersburg, PA 17236
717-328-9400
Ski school, night skiing, snowboard rental
25% most difficult, 53% more difficult, 22% easier, 100% snowmaking
Longest run: 4,900 ft., total slopes & trails: 17, vertical: 1,000 ft., mountain elevation: 1,935 ft.
chairlifts: 3 quad, 1 tow, 1 HS detach quad, 1 double
snow report: 717-328-9400

Ski Liberty
State 116 and Sanders Road
Fairfield, PA 17320
717-642-8282
717-642-8288 (hotel)
Ski school, night skiing, snowboard rental and halfpipe
30% most difficult, 40% more difficult, 30% easier, 100% snowmaking
Longest run: 5,300 ft., total slopes & trails: 15, vertical: 600 ft., mountain elevation: 1,186 ft.
chairlifts: 3 quad, 3 double, 1 J-bar, 1 handle tow
snow report: 800-829-4766

Skiing

Ski Roundtop
925 Roundtop Road
Lewisberry, PA 17339
717-432-9631
Ski school, night skiing, snowboard rental, halfpipe, and park
35% most difficult, 30% more difficult, 35% easier, 100% snowmaking
Longest run: 4,100 ft., total slopes & trails: 14, vertical: 600 ft., mountain elevation: 1,355 ft.
chairlifts: 1 quad, 1 triple, 5 double, 2 pony, 2 J-bar
snow report: 800-767-4766

Blue Marsh
P.O. Box 477
Bernville, PA 19506
610-488-6399
610-488-6396
Ski school, night skiing, snowboard rental and halfpipe
25% most difficult, 50% more difficult, 25% easier, 100% snowmaking
Longest run: 3,500 ft., total slopes & trails: 11, vertical: 300 ft., mountain elevation: 580 ft.
chairlifts: 1 triple, 1 double, 1 T-bar, 1 handle tow
snow report: 610-488-6399 or 610-488-6396

Doe Mountain
R.D. 1, Box 388
Macungie, PA 18062
610-682-7108
610-682-7109

Ski school, night skiing, snowboard rental and halfpipe
30% most difficult, 40% more difficult, 30% easier, 100% snowmaking
Longest run: 4,700 ft., total slopes & trails: 12, vertical: 500 ft., mountain elevation: 1,100 ft.
chairlifts: 1 triple, 3 double, 2 rope, 1 T-bar
snow report: 800-282-7107 or 610-682-7107

Northwest
Edinboro Ski Area
Box 447
Edinboro, PA 16412
814-734-1641
Ski school, night skiing, snowboard rental
15% most difficult, 75% more difficult, 10% easier, 40% snowmaking
Longest run: 2,800 ft., total slopes & trails: 11, vertical: 320 ft., mountain elevation: 1,550 ft.
chairlifts: 2 T-bars, 1 poma, 1 handle tow
snow report: 814-734-1641

Southwest
Blue Knob Recreation, Inc.
P.O. Box 247
Claysburg, PA 16625
814-239-5111
814-239-8580 FAX
Cross country, ski school, night skiing, snowboard rental
38% most difficult, 33% more difficult, 29% easier, 90% snowmaking
Longest run: 2 miles, total slopes & trails: 21, vertical: 1,072 ft., mountain elevation: 3,152 ft.
chairlifts: 2 triple, 2 double, 3 platters
snow report: PA 800-822-3045; outside PA 800-458-3403

Skiing

Boyce Park Ski Area
675 Old Frankstown Road
Pittsburgh, PA 15239
412-733-4656
Cross country, ski school, night skiing, snowboard rental and halfpipe
60% more difficult, 40% easier, 100% snowmaking
Longest run: 1,200 ft., total slopes & trails: 9, vertical: 172 ft., mountain elevation: 1,272 ft.
chairlifts: 2 double, 2 poma
snow report: 412-733-4665

Hidden Valley
4 Craighead Drive
Hidden Valley, PA 15502
814-443-2600
Cross country, ski school, night skiing, snowboard rental
30% most difficult, 35% more difficult, 35% easier, 100% snowmaking
Longest run: 1 mile, total slopes & trails: 17, vertical: 610 ft., mountain elevation: 3,000 ft.
chairlifts: 1 quad, 2 triple, 3 double, 2 pony
snow report: 800-443-SKII

Seven Springs Resort
R.D. 1
Champion, PA 15622
814-352-7777
800-452-2223 Continental U.S.
Ski school, snowboard rental
15% most difficult, 45% more difficult, 40% easier, 95% snowmaking

Longest run: 1.25 miles, total slopes & trails: 31, vertical: 750 ft., mountain elevation: 2,990 ft.
chairlifts: 2 quad, 7 triple, 2 double, 7 rope
snow report: 800-523-7777

State Organizations

Pennsylvania Ski Area Operators Association
HC 1, Box 7
White Haven, PA 18661
717-443-7180
Association of state ski area operators.

Pocono Mountains Vacation Bureau
1004 Main Street
Stroudsburg, PA 18360
800-762-6667 or 717-424-6050
Recorded ski conditions, 717-421-5565. "Ski the Poconos" brochure.

National Organizations

NASTAR
c/o World Wide Ski Corporation
402 D-AABC
Aspen, CO 81611
303-925-7864
National standard recreational ski racing programs.

National Handicapped Sports
5932 Illinois Avenue
Orangeville, CA 95662
916-989-0402
Administers recreational and competitive handicapped ski programs and hosts U.S. Disabled Ski Team.

National Ski Areas Association
133 South Van Gordon Street, Suite 300
Lakewood, CO 80228
303-987-1111
National association of ski area operators.

National Ski Patrol System (NSPS)
133 South Van Gordon Street, Suite 100
Lakewood, CO 80228
303-988-1111

Professional Ski Instructors of America (PSIA)
133 South Van Gordon Street, Suite 100
Lakewood, CO 80228
303-987-9390
Represents professional ski instructors.

70+ Ski Club
104 East Side Drive
Ballston Lake, NY 12019
518-399-5458
International ski club for skiers over seventy.

Ski Industries America
8377-B Greensboro Drive
McLean, VA 22102
703-556-9020
Association of ski product manufacturers.

SkiWee
1881 Ninth Street, Suite 335
Boulder, CO 80302
303-440-3636
Ski instruction program for children.

U.S. Recreational Ski Association
P.O. Box 25469
Anaheim, CA 92825-5469
714-634-1050
National recreational ski consumer organization.

U.S. Ski Association/U.S. Ski Team
P.O. Box 100, 1500 Kearns Boulevard
Park City, UT 84060
801-649-9090

CROSS-COUNTRY AREAS

Cross-country skiing rates tops as aerobic exercise and provides an unparalleled winter experience for those craving surcease from the multitudes congesting downhill ski areas on popular winter weekends. For all its allure, cross-country skiing in Pennsylvania is almost entirely dependent on the whims of Mother Nature. If she has been bountiful, the many choices include numerous rail trails, Allegheny

National Forest, state parks and forests, and cross-country areas complete with rentals, ski school, groomed and patrolled trails, food, and shelter.

Cross-country trails are traditionally measured in kilometers, with one kilometer (km) equaling .62 mile.

Northeast

Callender's Windy Acres Farm and Cross Country Skiing
R.D. 2, Box 174
Thompson, PA 18465
717-727-2982
A maple-sugaring operation, this farm has 10 kilometers of groomed trails, rentals, and a snack shack.

Cherry Ridge Farm Cross-Country Touring Center
Gallagher Road, R.D. 1, Box 489
Tobyhanna, PA 18466
717-676-4904
Rentals; trails in nearby state park, forest, and game lands; rental snowshoes; retail shop; guide service.

Crystal Lake Ski Center
R.R. 1, Box 308
Hughsville, PA 17737
717-584-2698
One of the best, with more than 30 kilometers of groomed and 10 kilometers of back-country trails designed for all levels of skiing. Machine grooming, set track, 3 kilometers of snowmaking, ski patrol, ski school, rentals, lodging, meals, and ski-in cabins.

Hanleys Happy Hill
Eagles Mere, PA 17731
717-525-3461
Another winner, with 50+ kilometers of groomed, set track plus ski patrol, back-country skiing, ski school, rentals, lodging, warm-up, and refreshment area.

Inn at Starlight Lake
P.O. Box 27
Starlight, PA 18461
800-248-2519 in all but 717 area codes or 717-798-2519
Charming turn-of-the-century country inn with an excellent dining room and skiing for both guests and nonguests. Rentals, 15 kilometers of groomed and set track, PSIA ski school, ski patrol, ski shop, and "Brown Bag" room.

North Central
Stone Valley Recreation Area
Bookstore Building
University Park, PA 16802
814-863-0762
On State 26 south, 11 miles from Pine Grove Mills. Heated rental cabins, 16 kilometers of groomed trails and 16 kilometers of backcountry, ice skating, and ice fishing.

Southwest
Hidden Valley Nordic Center
4 Craighead Drive
Hidden Valley, PA 15502
414-443-2600
Rentals, 50 kilometers of groomed trails, PSIA instructors, retail shop, child care, ski patrol.

Skiing

For More Information

For *Cross-country Skiing in Pennsylvania State Parks and Forests*, a twelve-page booklet listing locations, length of trails, and descriptions, contact:
Pennsylvania Bureau of State Parks
P.O. Box 8551
Harrisburg, PA 17105-8551
800-63-PARKS

For Pennsylvania Rails-to-Trails, contact:
Rails-to-Trails Conservancy, Pennsylvania Chapter
105 Locust Street
Harrisburg, PA 17101
717-238-1717

For information on cross-country skiing in Allegheny National Forest, send for *Discover the Allegheny National Forest Region*, an all-season, all-activities map, from:
Northern Alleghenies
315 Second Avenue
P.O. Box 804
Warren, PA 16365
800-624-7802 (eastern states) or 814-726-1222 (Warren County)

For maps of specific trails (Deerlick, Laurel Mill, Hearts Content, or Westline), contact:
Allegheny National Forest
P.O. Box 847
Warren, PA 16365
814-723-5150

Cross Country Ski Areas Association
259 Bolton Road
Winchester, NH 03470
603-239-4341
National organization of cross-country ski areas. Publishes *The Best of Cross-Country Skiing,* a how-to and where-to guide for the United States and Canada (fee).

9 SOURCES OF INFORMATION

For a state travel guide and official PennDOT highway map, contact:
Bureau of Travel Marketing
Pennsylvania Department of Commerce
800-VISIT PA

PENNSYLVANIA WELCOME CENTERS

Pennsylvania Turnpike

Sideling Hill Welcome Center
Mile marker 172
Waterfall

Zelienople Welcome Center
Zelienople Service Plaza
Rochester

Pennsylvania Outdoor Activity Guide

Neshaminy Welcome Center (westbound)
North Neshaminy Service Plaza
Trevose

I-70
Warfordsburg Welcome Center, westbound
First rest area, .5 mile west of Pennsylvania/Maryland border
Claysville Welcome Center (eastbound)
.5 mile west of exit 2 (anticipated opening fall 1995)

I-78
Easton Welcome Center
1400 Cedarville Road
Easton

I-79
Kirby Welcome Center (northbound)
5 miles north of Pennsylvania/West Virginia border
Edinboro Welcome Center (southbound)
First rest area south of Edinboro exit

I-80
West Middlesex Welcome Center (eastbound)
First rest area, .5 mile east of Pennsylvania/Ohio border

I-81
Lenox Welcome Center (southbound)
First rest area south of Lenox, exit 64
State Line Welcome Center (northbound)
First rest area, 1.5 miles north of Pennsylvania/Maryland border

Sources of Information

I-83

Shrewsbury Welcome Center (northbound)
First rest area, 1.5 miles north of Pennsylvania/Maryland border

I-95

Linwood Welcome Center (northbound)
First rest area, .5 mile north of Pennsylvania/Delaware border

REGIONAL TOURIST PROMOTION AGENCIES

Northeast

Columbia-Montour Tourist Promotion Agency, Inc.
121 Paper Mill Road
Bloomsburg, PA 17815
800-VISIT-10 or 717-784-8279
Columbia and Montour Counties

Endless Mountains Visitors Bureau
R.R. 6, Box 132A
Tunkhannock, PA 18657-9232
800-769-8999 or 717-836-5431
Bradford, Sullivan, Susquehanna, and Wyoming Counties

Pennsylvania's Northeast Territory Visitors Bureau
Airport Aviation Center, Hangar Road
Avoca, PA 18641
800-245-7711 or 717-457-1320
Lackawanna and Luzerne Counties

Pocono Mountains Vacation Bureau
1004 Main Street
Stroudsburg, PA 18360
800-762-6667 or 717-424-6050
Carbon, Monroe, Pike, and Wayne Counties

Schuylkill County Visitors Bureau
1440 Mahantongo Street
Pottsville, PA 17901
800-765-7282 or 717-622-7700

Southeast

Bucks County Tourist Commission, Inc.
P.O. Box 912, Dept. 56
Doylestown, PA 18901
800-836-2825 or 215-345-4552

Chester County Tourist Bureau
601 Westtown Road, Suite 170
West Chester, PA 19382-4536
800-228-9933 or 610-344-6365

Delaware County Convention & Visitors Bureau, Inc.
200 East State Street, Suite 100
Media, PA 19063
800-343-3983 or 610-565-3679

Lehigh Valley Convention & Visitors Bureau, Inc.
P.O. Box 20785
Lehigh Valley, PA 18002-0785
800-747-0561 or 610-882-9200
Lehigh and Northampton Counties

Sources of Information

Philadelphia Convention & Visitors Bureau
1515 Market Street, Suite 2020
Philadelphia, PA 19102
800-321-WKND or 215-636-1666
Philadelphia County

Valley Forge Convention & Visitors Bureau
600 West Germantown Pike
Plymouth Meeting, PA 19462
610-834-1550
Montgomery County

North Central

Cameron County Tourist Promotion Agency
P.O. Box 118
Driftwood, PA 15832
814-546-2665

Centre County Lion Country Visitors & Convention Bureau
1402 South Atherton Street
State College, PA 16801
800-358-5466 or 814-231-1400

Clinton County Tourist Promotion Agency, Inc.
Courthouse Annex, 151 Susquehanna Avenue
Lock Haven, PA 17745
717-893-4037

Elk County Recreation & Tourist Council, Inc.
141 Main Street, P.O. Box 35
Ridgway, PA 15853
814-772-5502

Pennsylvania Outdoor Activity Guide

Lycoming County Tourist Promotion Agency
454 Pine Street
Williamsport, PA 17701
800-358-9900 or 717-326-1971

Magic Forests of West Central Pennsylvania Tourism & Travel Bureau
R.R. 5, Box 47
Brookville, PA 15825
800-348-9393 or 814-849-5197
Butler, Clearfield, Clarion, and Jefferson Counties

Potter County Recreation, Inc.
P.O. Box 245
Coudersport, PA 16915-0245
814-435-2290 or 814-435-8230

Seneca Highlands Tourist Association, Inc.
P.O. Drawer G
Custer City, PA 16725
814-368-9370
McKean County

Susquehanna Valley Visitors Bureau
219D Hafer Road, P.O. Box 268
Lewisburg, PA 17837
800-458-4748 or 717-524-7234
Union, Northumberland, and Snyder Counties

Tioga County Tourist Promotion Agency
114 Main Street
Wellsboro, PA 16901
800-332-6718 (in PA) or 717-724-0635 (out of state)

Sources of Information

South Central

Cumberland Valley Visitors' Council
565 Lincoln Way East, P.O. Box 394
Chambersburg, PA 17201
717-261-1200
Franklin County

Gettysburg Travel Council, Inc.
35 Carlisle Street
Gettysburg, PA 17325
717-334-6274
Adams County

Harrisburg-Hershey-Carlisle Tourism & Convention Bureau
114 Walnut Street, P.O. Box 969
Harrisburg, PA 17108-0969
800-995-0969 or 717-232-1377
Cumberland and Dauphin Counties

Juniata-Mifflin County Tourist Promotion Agency
19 South Wayne Street
Lewistown, PA 17044
717-248-6713

Lebanon Valley Tourist and Visitors Bureau
625 Quentin Road, P.O. Box 329
Lebanon, PA 17042
717-272-8555
Lebanon County

Pennsylvania Dutch Convention & Visitors Bureau
501 Greenfield Road
Lancaster, PA 17601
800-735-2629 or 717-299-8901
Lancaster County

Perry County Tourist & Recreation Bureau
Courthouse, Center Square, P.O. Box 447
New Bloomfield, PA 17068
717-582-2131

Reading & Berks County Visitors Bureau
P.O. Box 6677
Wyomissing, PA 19610
800-443-6610 or 610-375-4085

York County Convention & Visitors Bureau
One Market Way East
York, PA 17401
800-673-2429 or 717-848-4000

Northwest

Crawford County Tourist Association
969 Park Avenue
Meadville, PA 16335
800-332-2338 or 814-333-1258

Forest County Tourist Promotion Agency
P.O. Box 608
Tionesta, PA 16353
800-222-1706 (in PA) or 814-927-8818 (out of state)

Sources of Information

Lawrence County Tourist Promotion Agency
Shenango Street Station
138 West Washington Street
New Castle, PA 16010
412-654-5593

Mercer County Tourist Agency
One West State Street
Sharon, PA 16146
800-637-2370 or 412-981-5880

Northern Alleghenies
315 Second Avenue, P.O. Box 804
Warren, PA 16365
800-624-7802 (15 eastern states) or 814-726-1222
Warren County

Tourist & Convention Bureau of Erie County
1006 State Street
Erie, PA 16501
814-454-7191

Venango County Area Tourist Promotion Agency
213 12th Street, P.O. Box 28
Franklin, PA 16323
800-776-4526 or 814-432-8005

Southwest

Armstrong County Tourist Bureau
402 East Market Street
Kittanning, PA 16201
412-548-3226

Pennsylvania Outdoor Activity Guide

Beaver County Tourist Promotion Agency
215B Ninth Street
Monaca, PA 15061
800-564-5009 (in area code 412), 800-342-8192 or 412-728-0212 (otherwise)

Bedford County Tourist Promotion Agency, Inc.
137 East Pitt Street
Bedford, PA 15522
800-765-3331 or 814-623-1771

Cambria County Tourist Council, Inc.
111 Market Street
Johnstown, PA 15901
800-237-8590 (PA, MD, OH) or 814-536-7993 and 814-539-3838 (elsewhere)

Convention & Visitors Bureau of Blair County
1231 Eleventh Avenue
Altoona, PA 16601
800-84-ALTOONA or 814-943-4183

Fulton County Tourist Promotion Agency
P.O. Box 141
McConnellsburg, PA 17233
717-485-4064

Greater Pittsburgh Convention & Visitors Bureau, Inc.
Four Gateway Center, Suite 514
Pittsburgh, PA 15222
800-366-0093 or 412-281-7711
Allegheny County

Sources of Information

Huntingdon County Tourist Promotion Agency
241 Mifflin Street
Huntingdon, PA 16652
814-643-3577

Indiana County Tourist Bureau, Inc.
1019 Philadelphia Street
Indiana, PA 15701
412-463-7505

Laurel Highlands, Inc.
Town Hall, 120 East Main Street
Ligonier, PA 15658
800-925-7669 or 412-238-5661
Fayette, Greene, Somerset, and Westmoreland Counties

Washington County Tourism
144 A McClelland Road
Canonsburg, PA 15317
800-531-4114 or 412-746-2333

INDEX

ADVICE
    Camping, 23–24
    Canoe Safety, 91–92
    Hiking, 20–22
    Whitewater Safety, 94–95
    Wildlife and insects, 22–23
AGENCIES, STATE
    Bicycling, 61
    Hiking, 25–26
    Horseback Riding, 81–82
    Paddle Sports, 98–100
ASSOCIATIONS. *See* CLUBS, ASSOCIATIONS, and ORGANIZATIONS

BALLOONING
    About, 157–158

Agencies, State, 61
Associations, 162–163
Special events
    Balloon Quest, New Castle, 163
    Fall Pumpkin Fest Hot Air Balloon Rally, Conneaut Lake Park, 164
    Shawnee Autumn Hot Air Balloon Festival, Shawnee-on-Delaware, 164
    Thurston Classic, sites vary, 164
Tour operators
    AAA Sky Ads, Tarentum, 161

Index

Adventures Aloft, Inc., Ephrata, 160
Aerial Adventures Over Pittsburgh, Inc., Venetia, 162
Balloonair, Villanova, 158
Ballooning, Inc., Upper Black Eddy, 158
Blue Dragon Balloons, North Wales, 159
Color the Sky, Doylestown, 159
Dillon Hot Air Balloon Service, Inc., Camp Hill, 161
Fantasy Flights, Center Valley, 161
Flights Aloft, Quakertown, 159
Keystone State Balloon Tours, Inc., Pipersville, 159
Lancaster Hot Air Balloons, Inc., Lancaster, 161
Lollipop Balloon, Chester, 159
Magical Mystery Flights, Media, 160
North Central area, 160
Pine Creek Hot Air Balloon Adventures, Cammal, 160
Ragge & Willow Enterprises, Inc., Greensburg, 162
Silver Lining Balloon Adventures, Harrisburg, 161
South Central area, 160–161
Southeast area, 158–160
Southwest area, 161–162
U.S. Hot Air Balloon Team, 160
Windswept Adventures, Ligonier, 162

BICYCLING
Advocacy Groups, State, 63–64
Associations, 62–63
Maps, Regional Tour, 51–52
Outfitters
　Blue Mountain Sports & Wear, Jim Thorpe, 52
　Camelback Ski Area/Alpine Slide, Tannersville, 52
　Country Pedal'rs Bicycle Touring, Somerset, 54
　Lancaster Bicycle Touring, Inc., Strasburg, 53–54
　Laurel Highlands River Tours, Ohiopyle State Park, Ohiopyle, 55
　Lumberville Store Bicycle Rental Co., Lumberville, 53
　McBeth's Cabins, Cooksburg, 53

201

Pennsylvania Outdoor Activity Guide

Mount Gretna Mountain Bikes, Ltd., Lebanon, 54
Mountain Streams, Ohiopyle, 55
Ohiopyle Trading Post, Ohiopyle, 55
Pocono Whitewater Mountain Bike Tours, Jim Thorpe, 52–53
River Sport Outfitters, Confluence, 55
Shadyside Mountain Bike Rental Center, Ligonier, 55
Shank's Mare, York, 54
Spoked Wheelz, Ohiopyle, 56
Vermont Bicycle Touring, Bristol, VT, 54
White Water Adventurers, Ohiopyle, 56
Whitewater Challengers Outdoor Adventure Center, White Haven, 53
Wilderness Voyageurs, Inc., Ohiopyle, 56
Youghiogheny Outfitters, Ohiopyle, 56
Regulations, 33–34
Road numbering system, 34
Special events
  Annual Lake Nockamixon Century, Horsham, 61
  Annual Mexican Metric Century, Horsham, 57
  Battle of Gettysburg Weekend Ride, Gettysburg, 56–57
  Blue and Grey Rally, Gettysburg College, 58
  Brandywine Tour, Delaware Valley, 60
  Covered Bridge Metric Century, Lancaster, 59
  Freedom Valley Bike Ride, 57
  The Great Ride, Pittsburgh, 59
  Horse Farm Tour, Hanover, 57
  Jim Thorpe Mountain Bike Weekend, Lititz, 58
  KAMEL (Kutztown and Millersville Eastern Loop), 58
  Labor Day Century, Hanover, 60
  Mon Valley Century, Pittsburgh, 59
  No Baloney Century, Lebanon Valley, 60
  Pixton Memorial Poker Ride, Horsham, 57
  River's Edge Century, Philadelphia, 60
  Sid Lustig Memorial Century, Harrisburg, 61

Index

Lehigh County Velodrome, Trexlertown, 58
Tour de Christiana, Christiana, 60
Tour de Toona, Altoona, 59
State parks
  Northeast, 35
  Northwest, 38–39
  South Central, 37–38
  Southeast, 35–37
  Southwest, 39–40
Tours/Accommodations, 62
Trails
  Allegheny Highlands Trail, Somerset, 48–49
  Allegheny National Forest, Warren, 45
  Allegheny River Trail, Franklin, 47
  Armstrong Trail, Kittanning, 49
  Conewago Trail, Lancaster, 46
  Endless Mountain Riding Trail, Montrose, 42
  Fairmont Park Bikeway, Philadelphia, 43
  Gettysburg National Military Park, Gettysburg, 40–41
  Ghost Town Trail, Indiana, 49
  Great Shamokin Path, Rural Valley, 49–50

Iron Horse Trail, Blain, 46
Lehigh Gorge State Park, Weatherly, 35
Lower Trail, Hollidaysburg, 50
Montour Trail, Pittsburgh, 50–51
Moraine State Park, Portersville, 39–40
Nockamixon State Park, Quakertown, 36
North Central region, 45
Northeast region, 42–43
Northwest region, 47–48
O&W Road Trail, Clifford, 42
Ohiopyle State Park, Ohiopyle, 40
Oil Creek State Park, Oil City, 38
Pine Gove Furnace State Park, Gardners, 37
Presque Isle State Park, Erie, 39
Ridley Creek State Park, Media, 36
Samuel Justus Recreational Trail, Seneca, 48
Schuylkill Trail (Philadelphia to Valley Forge Bikeway), Norristown, 43–44
South Central region, 47
Southeast region, 43–44
Southwest region, 48–51

State Forest and game land trails, 34
Stavich Bicycle Trail, Lowellville, OH, 48
Stony Valley Railroad Grade, Harrisburg, 46–47
Struble Trail, West Chester, 44
Swatara State Park, Grantville, 38
Switchback Railroad Trail, Jim Thorpe, 43
Towpath Bike Trail, Palmer, 44
Tyler State Park, Newtown, 37
Valley Forge National Historical Park, Valley Forge, 41–42
Williamsport and Lycoming Creek Bikeways, Williamsport, 45

BIRDING
Eagle viewing, Susquehanna River, 146
Organizations, 154–156
Sites
Beechwood Farms Nature Reserve, Pittsburgh, 152–153
Brucker Great Blue Heron Sanctuary of Thiel College, Greenville, 147
Bucks County, Doylestown, 142
Dorflinger-Suydam Wildlife Sanctuary, White Mills, 136–137
Erie National Wildlife Refuge, Guys Mills, 147–148
Grey Towers National Historic Landmark, 137–138
Hawk Mountain Sanctuary Association, 142–144
John J. Tyler Arboretum, Media, 142
John Heinz National Wildlife Refuge at Tinicum, Philadelphia, 139–140
Lacawac Sanctuary, 138–139
Middle Creek Wildlife Management Area, Kleinfeltersville, 144–146
Mill Grove, Audubon, 140–142
Moraine State Park, Portersville, 153–154
Presque Isle State Park, Erie, 148–149
Pymatuning State Park, Jamestown, 150–152
Tours, 156

Index

BOATING, STILL-WATER, 96–97

CLUBS, ASSOCIATIONS, and ORGANIZATIONS
 Ballooning, 162–163
 Bicycling, 61–64
 Birding, 154–156
 Cross Country Skiing, 188
 Hang gliding, 169
 Hiking, 26–30
 Horseback Riding, 82–83
 Orienteering, 31
 Paddle Sports, 97–98
 Polo Clubs, 84
 Rail Trails, 30
 Soaring, 166–167

EQUESTRIAN EVENTS. *See* HORSEBACK RIDING

FISHING
 Access to non-State areas, 131–133
 By Boat, 122
 Charters
  Tourist and Convention Bureau of Erie County, Erie, 130
  Trophy Guide Service, Huntingdon, 130
  Yocum's Professional Guide Service, Huntingdon, 130
 Fee fishing
  Arrowhead Springs, Newmanstown, 127
  Big Brown Fish and Pay Lake, Effort, 126
  Cedar Hollow Farm, Laceyville, 126
  DJ's Pay Lake, Rural Valley, 127
  Lake Tobias Wildlife Park, Halifax, 127
  Limestone Springs Fishing Preserve, Richland, 127
  Northeast region, 126
  Seghi's Five Lakes, Smithfield, 128
  South Central region, 127
  Southwest region, 127–128
 Fish for Free Days, 116–117
 Game fish
  Chain Pickerel, 119
  Largemouth bass, 117
  Muskie, 118
  Northern pike, 119
  Sauger, 120
  Shad, 120–121
  Smallmouth bass, 117
  Striped bass, 117–118
  Walleye, 119–120
 Guide services
  Allegheny Outdoors Guide Service, Bradford, 129
  Bill's Guide Service, Lake Ariel, 128

McConnell's Outdoor
  Adventures,
  Waterville, 129
North Central region,
  129
Northeast region, 128
Pecks Pond Rentals and
  Store, Dingmans
  Ferry, 128
South Central region,
  129–130
Tony Caps Guide
  Service, Dingmans
  Ferry, 128
Wolfe's General Store
  and Slate Run Tackle
  Shop, Slate Run,
  129
Yellow Breeches
  Outfitters, Boiling
  Springs, 129–130
Hatcheries, 122–126
License, trout/salmon,
  116
Optimum conditions, 115
Panfish, 121–122
Publications and
  information, 130–131
Salmon, 115
Seasons, trout/salmon,
  115–116
Streams, Freestone and
  Limestone, 114
Trout, 114–115
Yellow Breeches Creek,
  111–113
Special events

Eastern Sports, Boat,
  Camping, Travel and
  Outdoor Show,
  Harrisburg, 133
Forks of the Delaware
  Shad Fishing
  Tournament, Easton,
  134
Pennsylvania State
  Championship Fishing
  Tournament, Tidioute,
  134
Valley Forge Boat and
  Fishing Show, King of
  Prussia, 134
Valley Forge Sports,
  Recreation and
  Outdoor Show, King of
  Prussia, 134

GLIDERS AND SAILPLANES.
  See also SOARING
  About, 164–165
  Clubs and organizations,
    166–167

HANG GLIDING
  About, 168–169
  Organization, National, 169
HIKING
  Agencies, State, 25–26
  Clubs and organizations,
    26–30
  Information, specific trails,
    26–30

Index

Publications, 24–25
Rail trails
  Allegheny Portage
    Railroad Trail, 19
  Armstrong Trail,
    Clarion-Armstrong
    Counties, 19
  Clubs and organizations, 30
  Ghost Town Trail, Nanty Glo, 19
  Information, 30
  LeTort Spring Run Nature Trail, Carlisle, 19
  Pymatuning State Park Trail, Ohio border, 19
  Schuylkill River Trail, Philadelphia, 19
Trails
  Allegheny Portage Railroad Trail, 19
  Appalachian Trail, Boiling Springs/Whiskey Springs, 2–4
  Armstrong Trail, Clarion-Armstrong Counties, 19
  Baker Trail, Schenley, 6
  Black Forest Trail System, Slate Run, 7
  Bucktail Path, Sizerville State Park, 7
  Chuck Keiper Trail, Sproul State Forest, 7–8
  Conestoga Trail, Lancaster County, 8
  Darlington Trail, Sterretts Gap, 8–9
  Donut Hole Trail, Hyner Run State Park, 9
  Forbes Road Historic Trail, Cowans Gap State Park, 9–10
  Ghost Town Trail, Nanty Glo, 19
  Glacier Ridge Trail, Moraine State Park, 10
  Golden Eagle Trail, Cammal, 5–6
  Horse-Shoe Trail, Valley Forge National Historical Park, 10
  John P. Saylor Memorial Trail, Gallitzin State Forest, 10–11
  Laurel Highlands Hiking Trail, Laurel Ridge State Park, 11
  LeTort Spring Run Nature Trail, Carlisle, 19
  Lost Turkey Trail, Blue Knob State Park, 12
  Loyalsock Trail, Montoursville, 12
  Mason-Dixon Trail, Chadds Ford/Whiskey Springs, 12–13
  Mid State Trail System, Blackwell/US 22, 13
  North Country National Scenic Trail, Willow Bay Recreation Area, 13–14

Old Loggers Path,
    Ellenton, 14
Pinchot Trail System,
    Pocono Plateau, 14
Pymatuning State Park
    Trail, Ohio border, 19
Quehanna Trail, Parker
    Dam State Park, 15
Rachel Carson Trail,
    Harrison Hills
    Regional Park, 6
Schuylkill River Trail,
    Philadelphia, 19
Susquehannock Trail
    System, Denton Hill
    Ski Area, 15–16
Thunder Swamp Trail
    System, Delaware
    State Forest, 16
Tuscarora Trail,
    Harrisburg, 16–17
Warrior Trail,
    Greensboro, 17
West Rim Trail,
    Ansonia/Blackwell,
    17–18
HORSEBACK RIDING
  Agencies, State, 81–82
  Associations, 82–83
  Horse-Shoe Trail, Valley
    Vorge National
    Historic Park to
    Hershey, 67–68
  Hunt club information, 85
  Owner/rider facility
    Crooked Creek Horse
    Park, Kittanning, 82

Polo, 67
Polo Clubs, 84
Special events
  Devon Horse Show and
    Country Fair, Devon,
    80
  Handicapped Riders
    Event of the Devon
    Horse Show, Malvern,
    80
  Lancaster County Horse
    Farms Open House, 79
  Lawrence County
    Charity Horse Show,
    Volant, 80
  Pennsylvania Hunt Cup
    Races, Unionville, 81
  Pennsylvania National
    Horse Show,
    Harrisburg, 81
  Pennsylvania Special
    Olympics for
    Equestrians, Malvern,
    79
  Pony Express Ride,
    Kittanning, 80
  Radnor Hunt Fall Three-
    Day Event, Malvern, 81
  Radnor Hunt
    Steeplechase Racing
    for Open Space,
    Malvern, 79
Stables
  Ashford Farms, Miquon,
    70
  BarGee Farms, Allison
    Park, 77

Index

Brittany Common Horse Center, 72–73
Camp Allegheny, Stoystown, 77
Carson's Riding Stable, Cresco, 68
Centennial Hill Stables, Hollsopple, 77
Circle K Stables, Philadelphia, 70
Circle W Stables & Equestrian Park, Tionesta, 76
Deer Path Riding Stable, Inc., White Haven, 68
Endless Mountains Resort, Uniondale, 68
Fallen Timber Stables, Elizabeth, 78
Ferguson Farm, Blue Bell, 70–71
Gateway Stables, Kennett Square, 71
Gunsight Ranch, Mifflinburg, 73
Haycock Stables, Inc., Perkasie, 71
Heritage Acres, Dillsburg, 73
Horse Rentals, Harrisburg, 73
Inn at Meadowbrook, East Stroudsburg, 69
Knight's Point Stables, Newville, 73
Lower Hopewell Farms, Lititz, 74
Morning Star Stables, Library, 78
Mountain Creek Riding Stable, Cresco, 69
Mountain Trails Horse Center, Inc., Wellsboro, 72
National Riding Stable, Gettysburg, 74
Nemacolin Woodlands Equestrian Center, Farmington, 78
Nobodaddy Farm, Palmyra, 74
North Central, 72
Northeast, 68–70
Northwest and Allegheny National Forest, 76–77
Paradise Horses, Brookville, 72
Pine Crest Inc., Clarington, 72
Pinecrest Stables, Clarington, 76
Pocono Adventures, Jim Thorpe, 69
Pocono Manor Stables, Pocono Summit, 69
Robert O. Mayer Riding Academy, Inc., Glenshawn, 78
Rocking L Stables, Carlisle, 74
Seven Springs Resort, Champion, 79

209

Shadow Facs Farm,
  Waterford, 76
Shawnee Stables,
  Shawnee-on-Delaware,
  69
Smith Ranch, New
  Enterprise, 79
Snapfinger Farm,
  Chester Springs, 71
South Central region,
  72–76
Southeast region, 70–72
Southwest region, 77–79
Springhill Farm,
  Pottstown, 75
Tamiment Resort,
  Tamiment, 70
Thorncroft Equestrian
  Center, Malvern,
  71–72
Total Equine Learning
  Center, Lewisberry,
  75
Triple W Riding Stable,
  Inc., Honesdale,
  70
Venture Farms,
  Germansville, 75
Wet and Wild Acres,
  Brooksville, 77
Wind Swept Farms,
  Columbia, 75
Windy Ridge Acres,
  Newport, 76
Style, English and
  Western, 66–67

INFORMATION, SOURCES
  OF
Pennsylvania Welcome
  Centers, 189–191
Regional Tourist
  Promotion Agencies
  North Central, 193–194
  Northeast, 191–192
  Northwest, 196–197
  South Central, 195–196
  Southeast, 192–193
  Southwest, 197–199

ORGANIZATIONS. *See*
  CLUBS,
  ASSOCIATIONS, and
  ORGANIZATIONS
ORIENTEERING
  Clubs and organizations,
  31
  State Orienteering Sites, 20

PADDLE SPORTS
  Agencies, State and
  Federal, 98–100
  Charts, Navigation/
  Nautical, 101
  Clubs and organizations,
  97–98
  Maps and Guides, 100–101
  Outfitters and Liveries
  Adventure Sports Canoe
  and Raft Trips,
  Marshalls Creek, 102

Index

Allegheny Outfitters, Warren, 101
Allegheny River, 101
Anglers Roost and Hunter's Rest, Lackawaxen, 103
Belltown Canoe Rental, Sigel, 102
Blue Mountain Outfitters, Marysville, 107
Bubb's Canoe Rentals, Hughesville, 107
Canyon Cruise, Wellsboro, 106
Chamberlain Canoe Rentals, Minisink Hills, 103
Clarion River, 102
Cook Forest Canoe Livery, Cooksburg, 102
Delaware River, 102–104
Evergreen Outdoor Center, Harrisburg, 108
Foxburg Livery and Outfitters, Foxburg, 102
Hazelbaker Recreational Service, Perryopolis, 108
Indian Head Canoes, Newton, NJ, 103
Jim Thorpe River Adventures, Inc., Jim Thorpe, 105
Juniata River, 105
Kittatinny Canoes, Dingmans Ferry, 103
Lackawaxen River, 103, 105
Lander's Delaware River Trips, Narrowsburg, 104
Laurel Highlands River Tours, Ohiopyle, 108
Lehigh Rafting Rentals, Inc., White Haven, 105
Lehigh River, 105–106
Love's Canoe Rental and Sales, Ridgway, 102
Millers Canoe Rental, Millerstown, 105
Mountain Streams, Ohiopyle, 109
Northbrook Canoe Company, West Chester, 101
Ohiopyle Trading Post, Ohiopyle, 109
Pack Shack Adventure, Inc., 104
Pale Whale Canoe Fleet, Cooksburg, 102
Pecks Pond Rentals and Store, Dingmans Ferry, 107
Pine Creek, 106–107
Pine Creek Outfitters, Inc., Wellsboro, 106–107
Pinecrest, Clarington, 102

Pennsylvania Outdoor Activity Guide

Pocono Whitewater & Skirmish, Jim Thorpe, 105
Point Pleasant Canoe & Tube, Inc., Point Pleasant, 104
River Sport Outfitters, Confluence, 109
Scotty's Whitewater Raft Rides and Inner Tube Float Trips, Hawley, 105
Shawnee Canoe and Adventure Trips, Shawnee-on-Delaware, 104
Susquehanna River/Main Branch, 107–108
Susquehanna River/West Branch, 107
Swatara Creek (Harrisburg area), 108
Tee Pee Canoe Rental at Wysox, Towanda, 107
Tri-State Canoes and Boats, Matamoras, 104
Union Canal Canoe Rental, Annville, 108
Whitewater Adventurers, Inc., Ohiopyle, 109
Whitewater Challengers Outdoor Adventure Center, White Haven, 106
Whitewater Rafting Adventures, Inc., Albrightsville, 106
Wilderness Trekker, Orwigsburg, 106
Wilderness Voyageurs, Inc., Ohiopyle, 109
Wildware Outfitters, Harrisburg, 108
Youghiogheny River, 108–110
Youghiogheny Outfitters, Inc., Ohiopyle, 110
Rivers
  Brandywine River, 101
  Delaware River, 87–88
  Ohio River, 90–91
  Susquehanna River, 88–89
Safety, 91–92
Whitewater
  Clothing, 95–96
  Lehigh River Gorge, 93–94
  Pine Creek Gorge, 94
  Safety, 94–95
  Special conditions, 95
  Youghiogheny River, 92–93

SKIING, CROSS-COUNTRY
About, 184–185
Areas
  Callender's Windy Acres Farm and Cross Country Skiing, Thompson, 185

Index

Cherry Ridge Farm
   Cross-Country Touring
   Center, Tobyhanna,
   185
Crystal Lake Ski Center,
   Hughsville, 185
Hanelys Happy Hill,
   Eagles Mere, 186
Hidden Valley Nordic
   Center, Hidden Valley,
   186
Inn at Starlight Lake,
   Starlight, 186
North Central region,
   186
Northeast region,
   185–186
Southwest region, 186
Stone Valley Recreation
   Area, University Park,
   186
Association, 188
Maps and information, 187
SKIING, DOWNHILL
  About, 170–171
  Areas
   Alpine Mountain,
    Analomink, 172
   The Big Two—Big
    Boulder, Blakeslee,
    175–176
   The Big Two—Jack
    Frost, Blakeslee, 176
   Blue Knob Recreation,
    Inc., Claysburg, 180
   Blue Marsh, Bernville
    179

Blue Mountain,
   Palmerton, 173
Boyce Park Ski Area,
   Pittsburgh, 181
Camelback, Tannersville,
   173
Crystal Lake,
   Hughesville, 176
Doe Mountain,
   Macungie, 179–180
Edinboro Ski Area,
   Edinboro, 180
Elk Mountain, Union
   Dale, 171
Fernwood, Bushkill, 173
Hidden Valley, Hidden
   Valley, 181
Montage, Scranton,
   171–172
Mount Tone Ski Resort,
   Lake Como, 174
Mount Airy Lodge,
   Mount Pocono, 174
North Central region,
   176–178
Northeast region,
   171–176
Seven Springs Resort,
   Champion, 181–182
Shawnee Mountain,
   Shawnee-on-Delaware,
   174–175
Ski Denton,
   Coudersport, 177
Ski Liberty, Fairfield, 178
Ski Roundtop,
   Lewisberry, 179

Ski Sawmill, Morris, 177
South Central region, 178–180
Southwest region, 180–182
Split Rock Resort, Lake Harmony, 175
Spring Mountain Ski Area, Spring Mount, 172
Tanglwood, Tafton, 175
Tussey Mountain Ski Area, State College, 177–178
Whitetail Resort, Mercersburg, 178
Organizations, 182–184
SOARING. *See also* GLIDERS AND SAILPLANES
Clubs
Blue Mountain Aviation, Germansville, 167
Cloudniners, Elverson, 166
Country Aviation, Inc., Erwinna, 166
Keystone Gliderport, Julian, 166
Mid-Atlantic Soaring, Fairfield, 167
Philadelphia Glider Council, Inc., Ambler, 166
Soaring Society of Princeton University, Princeton, NJ, 166
South Central, 167
Southeast, 166
SPECIAL EVENTS
Ballooning, 163–164
Bicycling, 56–61
Equestrian (Horseback) Events, 79–81
Fishing, 133–134
STATE AGENCIES. *See* AGENCIES, STATE